# OFF-ROAD

# DECLARER PLAY

*Unusual Ways to Play a Bridge Hand*

## DAVID BIRD

MAST___ ___RESS
TO_____ ___NADA

**Master Point Press**
331 Douglas Ave.
Toronto, Ontario, Canada
M5M 1H2
(416) 781-0351
Website:         http://www.masterpointpress.com
Email:           info@masterpointpress.com

**Library and Archives Canada Cataloguing in Publication**

Bird, David, 1946-
   Off-road declarer play : unusual ways to play a bridge hand / written by David Bird.

ISBN-10  1-897106-19-X
ISBN-13  978-1-897106-19-8

   1. Contract bridge.  I. Title.

GV1282.3.B5916 2007          795.41'53          C2006-906533-0

Editor                              Ray Lee
Cover and interior design           Olena S. Sullivan/New Mediatrix
Interior format and copy editing    Suzanne Hocking

Printed in Canada by Webcom.

1 2 3 4 5 6 7          12 11 10 09 08 07

# CONTENTS

This book is dedicated to my friend and fellow bridge writer, Tim Bourke, who constructs two or three great deals every day and sends the best of them in my direction.

# CHAPTER 1

# FIGHTING YOUR WAY TO THE DUMMY

*From me to you*
The Beatles

When dummy is short of entries, or apparently contains no entries at all, you may need to employ special measures to reach it. In this chapter, we will see some useful techniques that can help you.

## LEADING ONE HONOR TO SET UP ANOTHER AS AN ENTRY

First, we will look at a play that is strangely difficult to spot at the table. Would you have made 4♡ here?

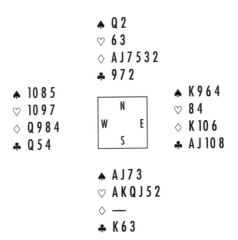

|            ♠ Q 2       |
|            ♡ 6 3       |
|            ◊ A J 7 5 3 2 |
|            ♣ 9 7 2     |

| WEST | NORTH | EAST | SOUTH |
|------|-------|------|-------|
|      |       |      | 1♡    |
| pass | 1NT   | pass | 4♡    |
| all pass |   |      |       |

West leads the ♡10 and you win with the ♡A. How will you play the contract?

Suppose your next move is a spade to dummy's queen. All will be well if West holds the ♠K. If he rises with the card, you will have three spade tricks and an entry to dummy's ◇A. You will make at least ten tricks. When East holds the ♠K, the situation will be less bright. He will win and return a second round of trumps, preventing a spade ruff. You can draw trumps and exit on the fourth round of spades, forcing the defenders to play a club for you, but you will still lose two spades and two clubs. What else can you try?

At Trick 2 you should lead the ♠J from your hand! As the cards lie, the defenders can do nothing. If East wins with the ♠K and returns another trump, you will win in your hand and draw the last trump. You can then cross to the ♠Q and discard a club loser on the ◇A. Finally, you will lead towards the ♣K for the contract. What if East chooses to hold up the ♠K? You will cash the ♠A and reach dummy with a spade ruff. You can then cash the ◇A for a club discard and lead towards the ♣K for an overtrick.

Here is another example of the play, this time in a notrump contract. Your objective on this occasion is not to reach a stranded winner, but to take a successful finesse.

```
              ♠ Q 7 2
              ♡ 9 8 3
              ◇ 7 5 4
              ♣ J 10 7 4
  ♠ 10 9 6 4 3            ♠ A J 8
  ♡ J 10 7 5      N       ♡ Q 6
  ◇ 9 6        W     E    ◇ Q J 10 8 3 2
  ♣ 6 5           S       ♣ K 8
              ♠ K 5
              ♡ A K 4 2
              ◇ A K
              ♣ A Q 9 3 2
```

| WEST | NORTH | EAST | SOUTH |
|------|-------|------|-------|
|      |       | 1◇   | dbl   |
| pass | 2♣    | pass | 3NT   |
| all pass |    |      |       |

West leads the ◇9, overtaken by East's ◇10. How will you tackle the notrump game?

If you simply play ace and another club, East will win and clear the diamond suit. You will then be one trick short. A better idea is to lead the ♠K at Trick 2. What can East do? If he wins with the ♠A and clears the diamonds, you can cross to the ♠Q to run the ♣J through East's ♣K. An overtrick will result. If, however, East holds up the ♠A to prevent you reaching dummy, you will have one spade trick in the bag and can afford to play clubs from your hand. You will score one spade trick, four red-suit winners and four club tricks.

What would have happened if South had headed for 5♣ instead of 3NT? With certain losers awaiting him in each major suit, declarer would need to reach the North hand to take a trump finesse. Not today! When the ♠K is led, East can simply hold up the ace. That's down one.

## 'UNNECESSARY FINESSE' TO GAIN AN ENTRY

Sometimes the straightforward entries to dummy will be insufficient to establish a side suit and reach the long cards. In that case, you may have to risk an otherwise unnecessary finesse, hoping to gain an extra entry. That's the only real chance on this slam deal:

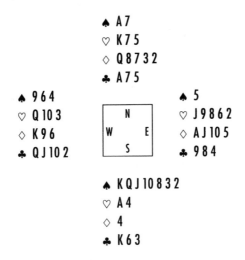

```
              ♠ A 7
              ♡ K 7 5
              ◇ Q 8 7 3 2
              ♣ A 7 5
   ♠ 9 6 4                    ♠ 5
   ♡ Q 10 3        N          ♡ J 9 8 6 2
   ◇ K 9 6    W         E     ◇ A J 10 5
   ♣ Q J 10 2       S          ♣ 9 8 4
              ♠ K Q J 10 8 3 2
              ♡ A 4
              ◇ 4
              ♣ K 6 3
```

| WEST | NORTH | EAST | SOUTH |
|------|-------|------|-------|
|  | 1◇ | pass | 1♠ |
| pass | 1NT | pass | 3♠ |
| pass | 4♣ | pass | 4NT |
| pass | 5♡ | pass | 6♠ |
| all pass | | | |

West leads the ♣Q against your ambitious small slam in spades. How will you play the contract?

You need to set up a long diamond, on which you can discard your club loser. Even if diamonds break 4-3, the three obvious entries to the dummy will not be enough to allow you to ruff three diamonds and then return to enjoy the established long card in the suit. Your best chance is to seek a fourth entry to dummy by finessing the ♠7.

You win the club lead with the king and play a diamond. East wins and returns a club to dummy's ace. You take your first diamond ruff with the ♠8 and, trying not to look worried, play the ♠2 to dummy's ♠7. Yes, it wins! You ruff a diamond with a high trump, everyone following, return to dummy with the ace of trumps and ruff another diamond high. You can then draw West's last trump, cross to dummy with the ♡K and discard your club loser on the established diamond.

Suppose you make the mistake of ruffing the first diamond with the ♠2 instead of the ♠8. A top-class West can then defeat you by inserting the ♠9 when you lead the ♠3 for the intended finesse of the ♠7. You would then have only one trump entry to dummy.

## Winning with an unnecessarily high card at Trick 1

When dummy contains a potential entry card in the suit that has been led, you can often promote its value by winning in your hand with an unnecessarily high card. Look at this deal:

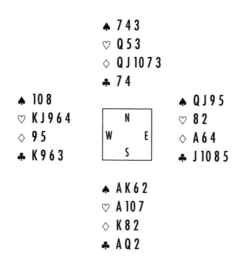

| WEST | NORTH | EAST | SOUTH |
|------|-------|------|-------|
|      |       |      | 2NT   |
| pass | 3NT   | all pass |   |

West leads the ♡6 against your game in notrump. You play low from dummy and East produces the ♡8. How will you play the contract?

Suppose your mind is on the bottle of wine awaiting you in the fridge and you win with the ♡10. You will go down. East will hold up the ◇A for two rounds and you will never reach the two good diamonds in dummy. The ♡Q will not provide an entry to dummy, because the ♡A and ♡K will win the next two rounds of the suit. Restricted to only two diamond tricks, you will be struggling to avoid down two.

To make the contract, you must win the first round of hearts with the ace. Dummy's ♡Q is now the second-ranked card in the suit and will provide an entry, provided West holds the ♡K as you expect. Let's say that East again holds up the ◇A for two rounds and then switches to the ♣J. You will win with the ♣A and lead a heart towards dummy. West will take his ♡K to stop you reaching dummy immediately, but the clubs will be safe with West on lead. Nine tricks will soon be yours.

Sometimes you employ this technique to give you a second entry to dummy in the suit that has been led.

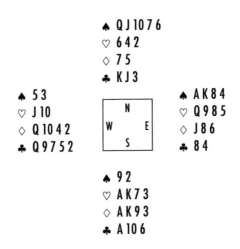

| WEST | NORTH | EAST | SOUTH |
|------|-------|------|-------|
|      |       |      | 1◇    |
| pass | 1♠    | pass | 2NT   |
| pass | 3NT   | all pass |   |

West leads the ♣5 against 3NT. You play low from dummy and East plays the ♣8. How will you give yourself the best chance of nine tricks?

If you win the first trick with the ♣10, you will go down against competent defenders. When you play the ♠9 next, East will allow this card to win. He will capture the second round of spades and you will then need two further entries to dummy — one to set up the spades and one to enjoy the established winners in the suit. With ♣K-J facing ♣A-6, only one entry to dummy will be available and you will go down.

See how much better you fare if you win the first round of clubs with the ace, an unnecessarily high card. East wins the second round of spades, as before, but you will now make the contract easily. You can win any red-suit switch from East and finesse the ♣J successfully. You can then clear the spade suit and use the ♣K as an entry to enjoy the long spades. Game made.

## UNBLOCKING AN HONOR FROM HAND AT TRICK 1

When your right-hand opponent has won the opening lead, it is sometimes beneficial to unblock the highest card from your hand. By doing so, you may promote dummy's top card into an extra entry.

```
              ♠ J 6 5
              ♡ 8 5 4
              ◇ Q J 10 8 6
              ♣ A 4
♠ K 10 8 4 2                    ♠ A 7
♡ K 6 3          N              ♡ J 10 9 7
◇ 9 3        W       E          ◇ K 7 4
♣ J 6 2          S              ♣ Q 9 7 5
              ♠ Q 9 3
              ♡ A Q 2
              ◇ A 5 2
              ♣ K 10 8 3
```

| WEST | NORTH | EAST | SOUTH |
|------|-------|------|-------|
|      |       |      | 1NT   |
| pass | 3NT   | all pass |   |

West leads the ♠4 against 3NT and East wins with the ace. How do you plan to make nine tricks?

If you follow with the ♠3 at Trick 1, you will not make the contract. When East returns the ♠7, West will duck if you play the ♠Q and win with the ♠K otherwise. You will not then be able to reach dummy with the ♠J to finesse in diamonds. If you continue with ace and another diamond, preserving the ♣K entry to enjoy the long diamonds later, the safe hand (East) will win. You will have only eight tricks, though; you will need a successful heart finesse to bring the total to nine and the king is offside. Nor will you fare any better by crossing to the ♣A to run the ◇Q. East will not cover, of course, and you will score the five diamond tricks you need only when East holds ◇K-x (or a singleton ◇K).

The correct technical move is to unblock the ♠Q from your hand at Trick 1. If the defenders continue spades, you will reach dummy with the ♠J. You can then run the ◇Q, followed by the ◇J. You cash the ◇A on the third round, picking up East's ◇K, and return to dummy with the ♣A to enjoy two further diamond tricks.

What if East switches to the ♡J at Trick 2? Best then is to rise with the ♡A and return a spade towards dummy's jack. West cannot continue hearts effectively from his side of the table and the game will be yours.

(Bridge is the strangest of games, as you have no doubt discovered already. At double-dummy, East can beat you by playing the ♠7 at Trick 1. By retaining the ♠A, he prevents you from using the ♠J as an entry to dummy.)

## SACRIFICING A TRICK TO REACH THE DUMMY

When reaching dummy may be worth two tricks, it can be smart business to sacrifice one trick to establish an entry. Look at this deal:

```
                        ♠ 6 3
                        ♡ A K 9 5 3 2
                        ◇ 10 9 3
                        ♣ 8 2
        ♠ Q 10 7 2              ┌─────────┐         ♠ J 9 8 5
        ♡ 10 8 4               │    N    │          ♡ Q J 7 6
        ◇ J 4             W │         │ E          ◇ Q 8 7
        ♣ Q 10 5 3            │    S    │          ♣ J 9
                             └─────────┘
                        ♠ A K 4
                        ♡ —
                        ◇ A K 6 5 2
                        ♣ A K 7 6 4
```

| WEST | NORTH | EAST | SOUTH |
|------|-------|------|-------|
|  |  |  | 1◇ |
| pass | 1♡ | pass | 3♣ |
| pass | 3♡ | pass | 3NT |
| all pass |  |  |  |

A small slam in diamonds would have succeeded as the cards lie. (You ruff a spade and discard two clubs on the high hearts. East can overruff the third round of clubs, but this absorbs his natural trump trick.) If you put 3NT on the floor instead, partner will not react kindly to any complaints about his bidding. How will you play when West leads the ♠2?

With dummy's heart winners currently inaccessible, you have only six tricks on top. Unless a defender holds ◇Q-J-x-x, you can establish two more tricks by playing ace and another diamond. However, the defenders will then clear two spade tricks and unless clubs break 3-3, you will not have time to set up a ninth trick. Is there anything better?

You must cut your way through to the dummy and the two precious jewels sitting there in the heart suit. Win the first round of spades and lead a low diamond towards dummy. You are hoping that West will hold at least one of the missing honors and that you can set up a dummy entry in the suit. Suppose West wins with the ◇J and clears the spade suit. You can then lead another low diamond, dummy's ◇10 forcing East's queen. The defenders can score a total of two spades and two diamonds, but nine tricks are yours. The ◇9 will provide an entry to the ace and king of hearts. You will make three tricks in diamonds and two tricks from each of the other suits. Sacrificing one of your four potential diamond tricks allowed you to reach the two heart honors in dummy.

Such sacrificial moves are sometimes available in the trump suit. Look at the spade suit here:

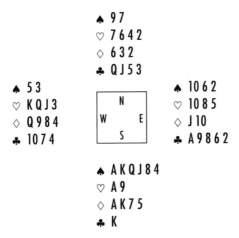

|  | ♠ 9 7 |  |
|---|---|---|
|  | ♡ 7 6 4 2 |  |
|  | ◇ 6 3 2 |  |
|  | ♣ Q J 5 3 |  |
| ♠ 5 3 |  | ♠ 10 6 2 |
| ♡ K Q J 3 | N | ♡ 10 8 5 |
| ◇ Q 9 8 4 | W    E | ◇ J 10 |
| ♣ 10 7 4 | S | ♣ A 9 8 6 2 |
|  | ♠ A K Q J 8 4 |  |
|  | ♡ A 9 |  |
|  | ◇ A K 7 5 |  |
|  | ♣ K |  |

| WEST | NORTH | EAST | SOUTH |
|---|---|---|---|
|  |  |  | 2♣ |
| pass | 2◇ | pass | 2♠ |
| pass | 2NT | pass | 3◇ |
| pass | 3♠ | pass | 4♠ |
| all pass |  |  |  |

West leads the ♡K. How will you play the spade game?

You win the heart lead with the ace. If your next move is to draw trumps, you are unlikely to make the contract unless diamonds break 3-3. A better idea is to lead the ♣K at Trick 2. If East holds up the ♣A, you will make the contract easily, losing just three tricks in the red suits. Let's suppose that East notes his partner's count signal of the ♣4 and captures the first round of clubs. He cashes the ♡10 and switches to the ◇J. What then?

Two club winners await you in the dummy and you can fight your way there in the trump suit. You win the diamond switch and lead the ♠4 to dummy's ♠7. East wins with the ♠10 and plays another diamond. You win with the ◇K and cross to dummy with the ♠9. You can then throw two losers on the ♣Q-J, return to the South hand with a high ruff and draw the last trump. Game made!

Let's wind the tape back to Trick 3. What would you do if East played a third round of hearts instead of switching to a diamond? You would have to ruff high, preserving your two trump spot cards as a means of entering the dummy.

## RUFFING HIGH TO PROMOTE A TRUMP ENTRY

When you want to reach dummy in the trump suit, it can assist your cause to ruff high in your own hand. The play is not easy to spot on this type of deal:

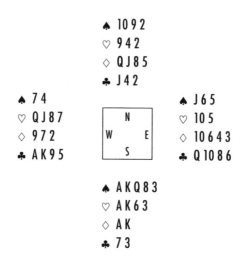

|                | ♠ 10 9 2 |       |         |
|                | ♡ 9 4 2  |       |         |
|                | ◇ Q J 8 5 |      |         |
|                | ♣ J 4 2  |       |         |
| ♠ 7 4          |          | N     | ♠ J 6 5 |
| ♡ Q J 8 7      | W        |     E | ♡ 10 5  |
| ◇ 9 7 2        |          | S     | ◇ 10 6 4 3 |
| ♣ A K 9 5      |          |       | ♣ Q 10 8 6 |
|                | ♠ A K Q 8 3 |    |         |
|                | ♡ A K 6 3 |     |         |
|                | ◇ A K    |       |         |
|                | ♣ 7 3    |       |         |

| WEST | NORTH | EAST | SOUTH |
|------|-------|------|-------|
|      |       |      | 2♣    |
| pass | 2◇    | pass | 2♠    |
| pass | 4♠    | all pass |   |

West leads the ♣A against your spade game and the defenders persist with two more rounds of clubs. How will you tackle the play?

A possible line is to ruff low and hope to escape for just one heart loser. (You would duck a heart, draw two rounds of trumps and play the ♡A-K. You would make the contract when hearts were 3-3 or a defender held four hearts and three trumps, allowing you to ruff the fourth heart.) As you can see, that line would fail here.

Let's try something different. You ruff the third round of clubs with the ace of trumps, aiming to use the ♠10-9 to provide an entry to the blocked diamond winners. You draw one round of trumps with the king, unblock the ace and king of diamonds and play a trump to dummy's ten. If East wins with the

♠J, he can do you no damage with his return. You will subsequently cross to the ♠10, drawing the last trump, and discard your two losing hearts on the ◇J-10. Nor will East fare any better by ducking the second round of trumps. Indeed, having arrived in dummy, you will discard both hearts and then draw his last trump, giving you an overtrick.

## UNBLOCKING A SPOT CARD TO CREATE AN EXTRA ENTRY

Even when you have several entries to dummy, it can be helpful to create one more. It is well known that with such as ♣A-Q-10-4 opposite ♣K-J-9-2, you can create extra entries to one hand or the other by overtaking honors. Here is a more subtle illustration of the technique:

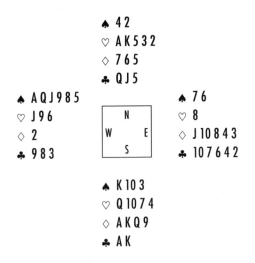

```
              ♠ 4 2
              ♡ A K 5 3 2
              ◇ 7 6 5
              ♣ Q J 5
♠ A Q J 9 8 5              ♠ 7 6
♡ J 9 6        N          ♡ 8
◇ 2        W       E      ◇ J 10 8 4 3
♣ 9 8 3        S          ♣ 10 7 6 4 2
              ♠ K 10 3
              ♡ Q 10 7 4
              ◇ A K Q 9
              ♣ A K
```

| WEST | NORTH | EAST | SOUTH |
|------|-------|------|-------|
| 2♠ | pass | pass | dbl |
| pass | 4♡ | pass | 4NT |
| pass | 5♡ | pass | 6NT |
| all pass | | | |

North shows two keycards in response to Roman Keycard Blackwood and South bids the small slam in notrump to protect his ♠K from the opening lead. How will you play this contract when West leads the ♣9?

Since you may eventually need to finesse in the diamond suit, you should pay attention to the entries to dummy. You win the club lead and cash the other club honor in your hand. You then lead the ♡7 to dummy's ace, carefully

retaining the ♡4 in case you should wish to cross to the ♡5 later. You cash the
♣Q, throwing a spade, and note that West follows suit. When you play a heart
to the queen, East surprises you by showing out. You are now close to a complete count on the defenders' hands. A diamond to the ace fills in the last piece
of the puzzle. Assuming West has the expected six spades for his weak two-bid,
he began with 6-3-1-3 shape and you will need to finesse in diamonds to score
four tricks with the jack and ten onside.

You lead the ♡10 to dummy's king, again preserving the ♡4, and lead a
diamond towards your hand. If East plays low, you will take a deep finesse of
the ◇9 with every confidence. If instead East inserts the jack or ten of diamonds, you will win and re-enter dummy for a further diamond play by overtaking the ♡4 with the ♡5.

## FORESEEING THE NEED FOR AN EXTRA ENTRY

Assessing how many entries to each hand you will need is a basic part of planning a contract. Many players would go down on the next contract. (It's true
that many more would correctly avoid bidding it!). See how you fare yourself.

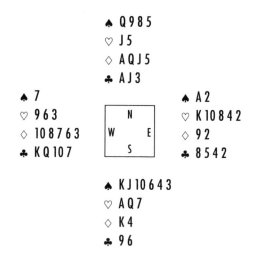

```
              ♠ Q 9 8 5
              ♡ J 5
              ◇ A Q J 5
              ♣ A J 3
    ♠ 7                      ♠ A 2
    ♡ 9 6 3        N         ♡ K 10 8 4 2
    ◇ 10 8 7 6 3   W    E    ◇ 9 2
    ♣ K Q 10 7         S     ♣ 8 5 4 2
              ♠ K J 10 6 4 3
              ♡ A Q 7
              ◇ K 4
              ♣ 9 6
```

| WEST | NORTH | EAST | SOUTH |
|------|-------|------|-------|
|      | 1NT   | pass | 3♠    |
| pass | 4♣    | pass | 4◇    |
| pass | 5◇    | pass | 6♠    |
| all pass | | | |

West leads the ♣K against your small slam. How will you play the contract?

You win with dummy's ♣A and recognize that you will need to dispose of your club loser before drawing trumps. Suppose, though, that you play the king, ace and queen of diamonds immediately. East will ruff the third round with the ♠2 and you will have to overruff. There is no quick entry to the dummy to play another diamond winner and you will go down one.

Since you will eventually have to take a winning heart finesse to make the contract, you should attempt it at Trick 2. The finesse wins and you then play the three top diamond honors. East ruffs the third round, as before, but now you have prepared an extra entry to dummy! You cash the ♡A and ruff a heart. When you play dummy's remaining diamond honor, East has to ruff with the ♠A. Your club loser goes away and the small slam is made.

**1**

♠ Q 5 3
♡ 10 3
◇ A Q 10 5 4 3
♣ 8 6

♠6 led

♠ K 10 7
♡ A J 7 5
◇ J 2
♣ A K 4 3

| WEST | NORTH | EAST | SOUTH |
|------|-------|------|-------|
|      |       |      | 1NT   |
| pass | 3NT   | all pass |   |

West leads the ♠6 against 3NT, East playing the ♠9. How will you play the contract?

**2**

♠ K 10 7 2
♡ 8 4
◇ 9 6 4 3
♣ 8 7 2

◇K led

♠ A
♡ A K J 10 9 3
◇ A 5 2
♣ A K 6

| WEST | NORTH | EAST | SOUTH |
|------|-------|------|-------|
|      |       |      | 2♣    |
| pass | 2◇    | pass | 2♡    |
| pass | 2NT   | pass | 3♡    |
| pass | 4♡    | all pass |   |

West leads the king of diamonds against your game in hearts. How will you play the contract?

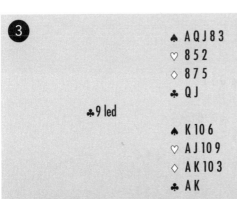

**3**

♠ A Q J 8 3
♡ 8 5 2
♢ 8 7 5
♣ Q J

♣9 led

♠ K 10 6
♡ A J 10 9
♢ A K 10 3
♣ A K

| WEST | NORTH | EAST | SOUTH |
|------|-------|------|-------|
|      |       |      | 2♣ |
| pass | 2♠ | pass | 2NT |
| pass | 6NT | all pass | |

West leads the ♣9 against your slam in notrump. How will you play the contract?

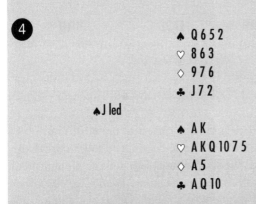

**4**

♠ Q 6 5 2
♡ 8 6 3
♢ 9 7 6
♣ J 7 2

♠J led

♠ A K
♡ A K Q 10 7 5
♢ A 5
♣ A Q 10

| WEST | NORTH | EAST | SOUTH |
|------|-------|------|-------|
|      |       |      | 2♣ |
| pass | 2♢ | pass | 2♡ |
| pass | 4♡ | pass | 6♡ |
| all pass | | | |

West leads the ♠J and you win with the ♠A. When you play the ace of trumps, the jack falls from West. How will you continue the play?

1

```
                    ♠ Q 5 3
                    ♡ 10 3
                    ◊ A Q 10 5 4 3
                    ♣ 8 6
    ♠ A J 8 6 2                      ♠ 9 4
    ♡ Q 8 6        ┌─────────┐       ♡ K 9 4 2
    ◊ 9 8          │    N    │       ◊ K 7 6
    ♣ J 9 5        │ W     E │       ♣ Q 10 7 2
                   │    S    │
                   └─────────┘
                    ♠ K 10 7
                    ♡ A J 7 5
                    ◊ J 2
                    ♣ A K 4 3
```

| WEST | NORTH | EAST | SOUTH |
|------|-------|------|-------|
|      |       |      | 1NT   |
| pass | 3NT   | all pass |   |

West leads the ♠6 against 3NT, East playing the ♠9. How will you play the contract?

Let's see what happens if you win the first trick with the ♠10. You run the ◊J and it wins, East holding up the ◊K in an attempt to kill dummy's diamond suit. A second diamond finesse loses and East returns his remaining spade. West will not allow the ♠Q to become an entry; if you play your ♠K on the second round, he will hold up the ♠A. Unable to enter the dummy, you will fall well short of your target.

A better idea is to win the first trick with an unnecessarily high card, the ♠K. This promotes dummy's ♠Q in value and it will now provide an entry. East ducks the ◊J as before and wins the second round of diamonds. You will win a heart or club return and lead a spade towards dummy, establishing the ♠Q as an entry. Nothing can prevent you from scoring five diamond tricks and making the contract.

♠ K 10 7 2
♡ 8 4
◇ 9 6 4 3
♣ 8 7 2

♠ J 6 4 3           ♠ Q 9 8 5
♡ 7 5               ♡ Q 6 2
◇ K Q J 8   **W    E**  ◇ 10 7
♣ J 9 4             ♣ Q 10 5 3

(N / S box center)

♠ A
♡ A K J 10 9 3
◇ A 5 2
♣ A K 6

| WEST | NORTH | EAST | SOUTH |
|------|-------|------|-------|
|      |       |      | 2♣    |
| pass | 2◇    | pass | 2♡    |
| pass | 2NT   | pass | 3♡    |
| pass | 4♡    | all pass |   |

West leads the ◇K against your heart game. How will you play the contract?

There is no entry to dummy for a trump finesse, but you have some chance of escaping a trump loser by laying down the ace and the king. If the ♡Q does not drop in two rounds, however, you are almost certain to go down, losing three subsequent tricks in the minor suits. What else can you try?

You should win the diamond lead and cash the ♠A. Next you play the ♡J from your hand. East now has two losing alternatives. If he refuses to win with the ♡Q, you will score six trump tricks to go with your four winners in the side suits. If instead East wins with the ♡Q, he will set up dummy's ♡8 as an entry. You will be able to cross to dummy and throw your club loser on the ♠K.

Dummy held only one side-suit winner on this deal, but it was still profitable to surrender a trump trick to reach it, since you were likely to have a trump loser anyway. You would play the same way with ♡A-K-Q-10-9-3. Since you might lose a trump trick to ♡J-x-x-x, you would unblock the ♠A and lead the ♡10 from your hand.

```
                    ♠ A Q J 8 3
                    ♡ 8 5 2
                    ◇ 8 7 5
                    ♣ Q J
  ♠ 9 7 5 2                        ♠ 4
  ♡ Q 7            ┌─────────┐     ♡ K 6 4 3
  ◇ Q 9 6 4        │ W   N  E│     ◇ J 2
  ♣ 9 8 3          │     S   │     ♣ 10 7 6 5 4 2
                   └─────────┘
                    ♠ K 10 6
                    ♡ A J 10 9
                    ◇ A K 10 3
                    ♣ A K
```

| WEST | NORTH | EAST | SOUTH |
|------|-------|------|-------|
|      |       |      | 2♣    |
| pass | 2♠    | pass | 2NT   |
| pass | 6NT   | all pass |   |

West leads the ♣9 against 6NT. How will you play the contract?

There are nine top tricks available outside the heart suit, so three heart tricks will give you the slam. Since you may need to finesse three times in hearts, you must look for three entries to dummy in the spade suit. After winning the club lead, you begin by leading the king of spades and overtaking with the ace. Everyone follows and you take your first heart finesse, the jack losing to the queen.

West returns another club and you win in hand. Your next play is to lead the ten of spades. When West follows, it is safe to overtake with dummy's queen. East shows out, but this causes no problems, because dummy's remaining ♠J-8 tenace lies over West's ♠9-7. A finesse of the ♡10 proves successful. You take the marked finesse of the ♠8, which is your third spade entry to the dummy, and cash dummy's last two spade winners. You then lead another heart, finessing for the third time, and pick up the three heart tricks that you need.

Suppose West had shown out on the second round of spades. In that case, you could not afford to overtake again, since it would establish a trick for East's ♠9-x-x-x. You would have to play low from dummy and cross to the ♠Q on the third round. After cashing the remaining spade honors, you would then have to hope that one more heart lead from dummy was enough to pick up the suit.

4

```
              ♠ Q 6 5 2
              ♡ 8 6 3
              ◊ 9 7 6
              ♣ J 7 2
  ♠ J 10 9 7              ♠ 8 4 3
  ♡ J          N          ♡ 9 4 2
  ◊ K 10 8 4  W   E       ◊ Q J 3 2
  ♣ 8 6 5 3      S         ♣ K 9 4
              ♠ A K
              ♡ A K Q 10 7 5
              ◊ A 5
              ♣ A Q 10
```

| WEST | NORTH | EAST | SOUTH |
|------|-------|------|-------|
|      |       |      | 2♣ |
| pass | 2◊ | pass | 2♡ |
| pass | 4♡ | pass | 6♡ |
| all pass |  |  |  |

North's 4♡ was an overbid. He should have continued with a second negative, intending to bid 4♡ on the next round. West leads the ♠J and you win with the ♠A. When you play the ace of trumps, the jack falls from West. How will you continue the play?

Dummy's ♡8-6 now represents a guaranteed entry to the blocked winner in spades. Once in dummy, you will be able to take a club finesse as well. To give yourself an extra chance, you should lead the ♣Q from your hand at Trick 3. If the defenders win with the ♣K, you can use the ♣J as an entry for the third spade trick and will avoid surrendering a trump trick. Let's say that East takes due note of his partner's ♣6 count signal and holds up the ♣K. What then?

You will need the ♣K to be onside. You cash your remaining spade honor and lead the ♡5 to dummy's ♡6. East wins with the ♡9 and returns a diamond. You rise with the ◊A and lead the ♡7 to dummy's ♡8. You can then discard your diamond loser on the ♠Q and take the club finesse. Justice is served, from your point of view at least, and you make the small slam.

**CHAPTER 2**

# ANTI-BLOCKING PLAYS

*Get out of my way*
The Uptones

The game of bridge offers many potential annoyances. High on the list is the situation where one of your suits is blocked, particularly if you don't notice it until too late! In this chapter, we will see some techniques that you can use to side-step an approaching blockage.

## SACRIFICE A TRICK TO AVOID A BLOCKAGE

We begin with a deal where it is within your power to prevent a blockage in the first place.

```
              ♠ 4 2
              ♡ 5 2
              ◇ A K 7 6 5 4 2
              ♣ 8 6
♠ 10 9 3                      ♠ Q J 8 7 5
♡ K 8 6          N            ♡ Q 9 7 4
◇ Q 3        W     E          ◇ 9
♣ K Q J 10 2      S           ♣ 9 7 3
              ♠ A K 6
              ♡ A J 10 3
              ◇ J 10 8
              ♣ A 5 4
```

| WEST | NORTH | EAST | SOUTH |
|------|-------|------|-------|
|      |       |      | 1NT   |
| pass | 3NT   | all pass |    |

How will you play 3NT when West leads the ♣K?

No major-suit switch will threaten you, so you should hold up the ♣A until the third round. You must then decide how to tackle the diamond suit. Suppose your first move is to lead the ◊J to dummy's ◊A. The ◊Q fails to appear on the first round and you will be forced to duck the second round of diamonds to avoid a blockage. Unfortunately for you, it will be West who produces the ◊Q. He will cash two more club winners and you will be down one.

To avoid the blockage that will arise when the ◊Q is doubleton, you must run the ◊J on the first round of the suit. You don't mind losing a diamond trick to East, because he is a safe hand. He will have no club to play, unless the suit is divided 4-4 and poses no problem. As the cards lie, the ◊J will win. Dummy's ◊A-K will take the next two rounds of the suit and no blockage will arise.

Bizarre as it may seem, you would make the same play (running the ◊J on the first round) even if dummy held the ◊3 in addition, giving you an 8-3 diamond fit. Failure to do so would leave the suit blocked if West held ◊Q-9.

## DISCARDING THE CARD THAT CAUSES A BLOCKAGE

Next we will see a couple of deals where you can arrange to throw away the card that threatens to cause a blockage. Test yourself on this spade slam:

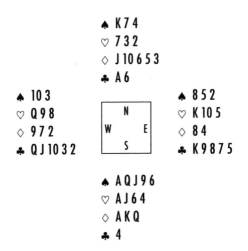

| WEST | NORTH | EAST | SOUTH |
|------|-------|------|-------|
| | | | 1♠ |
| pass | 2♠ | pass | 4NT |
| pass | 5♡ | pass | 6♠ |
| all pass | | | |

No bidding prizes for South, but maybe you can find a clever play in the 6♠ that he reached. How will you tackle the slam when West leads the ♣Q?

Five spades, five diamonds and two aces will add up to twelve tricks. The problem is that the diamond suit is blocked and you will need to use the third round of trumps as an entry to the long diamonds. Suppose you win the club lead and draw two rounds of trumps with the ace and the queen. Trumps will break 3-2, but you will have to play all three diamond honors in your hand while there is still a trump out. As the cards lie, East will ruff the third diamond and you will be a trick short.

Instead you must aim to discard one of the blocking diamond honors. Win the club lead with the ace and immediately play dummy's ♣6, throwing the ◇Q from your hand. Let's say that East wins the trick and switches to a heart. You will rise with the heart ace and draw two rounds of trumps with the ace and the queen. Since you have discarded one diamond honor, you now need to cash only two diamond honors in your hand. In other words, you do not need to lean on Lady Luck so hard! The defender with the last trump (East) does hold two diamonds, so all is well. You can then cross to dummy with a third round of trumps and cash the ◇J-10-6, throwing all three heart losers.

On the next deal, it is not at all easy to see how you might dispose of the blocking card in your hand.

```
              ♠ 9 6 4
              ♡ Q J 8 7
              ◇ 9 7 6 5 4 2
              ♣ —
  ♠ Q J 2                    ♠ A K 10 8 7 5
  ♡ 9 6 5 3        N         ♡ —
  ◇ J 8        W       E     ◇ Q 3
  ♣ 10 7 5 2       S         ♣ K Q 9 6 3
              ♠ 3
              ♡ A K 10 4 2
              ◇ A K 10
              ♣ A J 8 4
```

| WEST | NORTH | EAST | SOUTH |
|------|-------|------|-------|
|      |       |      | 1♡ |
| pass | 4♡ | 4♠ | 6♡ |
| all pass |  |  |  |

West leads the ♠Q, winning the first trick, and switches to the ♡3. What is your plan for the contract? (East will show out on the first round of trumps.)

You need the diamond suit to break 2-2, but that is not the end of the matter. You cannot simply play the ace-king of diamonds and draw trumps, ending in the dummy, because the ◇10 will block the suit. How can you dispose of the annoying ◇10? The only solution is to throw it away on the fourth round of trumps! This implies that you must take two spade ruffs in your own hand in order to leave yourself with one fewer trump than the dummy.

You play the ♡7 from dummy, since if East covers there will be no problem with the trump suit. When East shows out, you leave the lead in dummy. You ruff a second round of spades with the ♡A, cross to dummy with a finesse of the ♡8 and ruff dummy's last spade with the ♡K. You then cross your fingers (if that is your belief) and play the ace-king of diamonds. Both defenders follow and you overtake the ♡10 with the ♡J. You then draw West's last trump with dummy's ♡Q, discarding the blocking ◇10 at the same time. The slam is yours.

## DELAY THE UNBLOCKING DISCARD

Sometimes you cannot tell immediately whether or not you want to ditch a card that may cause a blockage:

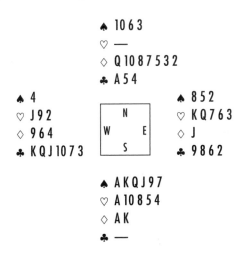

| WEST | NORTH | EAST | SOUTH |
|------|-------|------|-------|
| 3♣ | pass | 5♣ | 6♠ |
| pass | 7♠ | all pass | |

How will you play the grand slam when West leads the ♣K?

Suppose you win with the ♣A, throwing a heart, and try to ruff your remaining three heart losers. You use club ruffs as the entries for the first two heart ruffs and then cross to the ◊A to ruff your last heart loser. So far, so good. However, you will be stuck in dummy, forced to play a second round of diamonds. East will pounce with a trump and that will be down one.

A more obvious and better line of play is to rely on dummy's diamond suit. Let's say that you win the first trick with the ♣A. What should you throw from the South hand? Much of the time it would work well to throw a diamond honor. You could then play two rounds of trumps and cash your remaining diamond honor. Whenever the ◊J fell singleton or doubleton, you could reach dummy with the ♠10 and enjoy the rest of the diamonds. Such a line would not be a success, though, when the same defender held three trumps and ◊J-x-x.

To cater for all eventualities, you should delay your discard on the ♣A. You should ruff the first club and play two rounds of trumps, West showing out on the second round. Your main hope is that East holds at least two diamonds, allowing you to cash the ace and the king. When you play the ◊A, however, the ◊J falls from East. Excellent! You abandon diamonds for now, cross to the ♠10 and only then play the ♣A, throwing the blocking king of diamonds. The rest of dummy's diamond suit is yours and you make the grand slam.

## THROW THE BLOCKING CARD ON A DEFENDER'S WINNER

On the next deal, it is the defenders who create an unwanted blockage for you. Very well, let them assist you in relieving it!

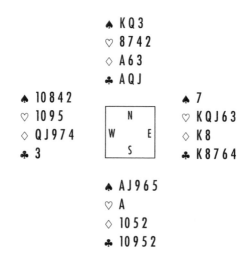

| WEST | NORTH | EAST | SOUTH |
|------|-------|------|-------|
|      |       | 1♡   | 1♠    |
| pass | 2♡    | pass | 2♠    |
| pass | 4♠    | all pass |   |

With four trumps in his hand, West rightly attacks in hearts rather than leading his singleton club. You win with the ace and draw trumps in four rounds. As you see, there is a potential blockage problem in the club suit. How do you plan to overcome it?

You lead a club to the ace at Trick 6 and continue with the queen of clubs. East cannot afford to duck both the queen and the jack of clubs, of course, or you will have ten tricks. His best defense is to win the second round of clubs, leaving the ♣J to block the suit. How will you play when he continues with the ♡K?

This is the position you have reached:

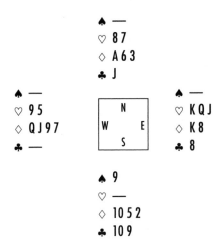

♠ —
♡ 8 7
◇ A 6 3
♣ J

♠ —          ♠ —
♡ 9 5        ♡ K Q J
◇ Q J 9 7    ◇ K 8
♣ —          ♣ 8

♠ 9
♡ —
◇ 10 5 2
♣ 10 9

When East returns the ♡K, you cannot afford to ruff because the club suit is blocked. You discard a diamond instead and East persists with the ♡Q. Again you discard a diamond loser. Now the defense has run out of steam. If East plays yet another heart winner, you will ruff in your hand and discard the blocking ♣J from dummy. The ♣10-9 will wrap up your game. If instead East switches to a diamond, you can win in the dummy and unblock the ♣J. You will have a ruffing entry to the South hand to enjoy your last club.

## AVOIDING A BLOCKAGE IN THE TRUMP SUIT

Let's end with two deals where you must avoid a blockage in the trump suit.

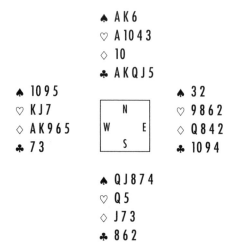

♠ A K 6
♡ A 10 4 3
◇ 10
♣ A K Q J 5

♠ 10 9 5
♡ K J 7
◇ A K 9 6 5
♣ 7 3

♠ 3 2
♡ 9 8 6 2
◇ Q 8 4 2
♣ 10 9 4

♠ Q J 8 7 4
♡ Q 5
◇ J 7 3
♣ 8 6 2

West leads the ◇K against 6♠ and continues with the ◇A, hoping to cause a problem by locking you in dummy. How will you continue?

Suppose you ruff the second diamond with dummy's ♠6. The trump suit will be blocked and you will run into exactly the sort of communication problem that West was hoping to cause. After cashing the ace and king of trumps, you would have no way to reach your hand safely to draw the last trump.

You should therefore ruff with dummy's ♠A at Trick 2, even though this may promote a trump trick for the defenders when trumps break 4-1. It is then an easy matter to play king and another trump, winning the second round in the South hand. Nothing can stop you from drawing the last trump and claiming twelve tricks. If you're that sort of person, you can point out to West that a black-suit switch at Trick 2 would have given you no chance at all.

On the next deal, too, there is a risk that the trump suit will become blocked.

```
                    ♠ A K Q J
                    ♡ K Q 10 3
                    ◇ A K Q 2
                    ♣ 6
   ♠ 10 7                              ♠ 9 6 5 3
   ♡ 2            ┌─────────────┐      ♡ J 8 7 5
   ◇ 9 6 3       │      N      │      ◇ J 7
   ♣ K Q J 10 7 5 4 │ W       E │      ♣ A 9 2
                    │      S      │
                    └─────────────┘
                    ♠ 8 4 2
                    ♡ A 9 6 4
                    ◇ 10 8 5 4
                    ♣ 8 3
```

| WEST | NORTH | EAST | SOUTH |
|------|-------|------|-------|
| 3♣ | dbl | 4♣ | pass |
| pass | dbl | pass | 4♡ |
| pass | 4NT | pass | 5◇ |
| pass | 6♡ | all pass | |

How will you play the heart slam when West leads the ♣K and continues with a second round of clubs?

Suppose you ruff with the ♡3 and continue with the king and queen of trumps. West will show out on the second round and East will refuse to cover the ♡10. You will be stuck in the dummy, unable to draw the last trump. When you switch to the side suits, East will ruff the third round of diamonds. Down one!

It is very unlikely that West holds ♡J-x-x-x. It is even more unlikely that you would begin with the king and ace of trumps, allowing you to pick up such a division. So, the ♡10 is of no value for finessing purposes and might well get in your way if you need to pick up ♡J-x-x-x from East. You should therefore dispose of it at Trick 2. Ruff the second round of clubs with the ♡10. When you continue with the king and queen of trumps, your reward will come. The way will be clear to finesse the ♡9. You can then draw East's last trump with the ♡A and claim the contract when the diamond suit comes in.

# UNBLOCKING ON THE THROW-IN CARD

A common type of end position is where you throw in a defender, forcing him to lead into a tenace. When this tenace is faced by a blocking card in the opposite hand, you may be able to discard it as you perform the throw-in. Look at this deal:

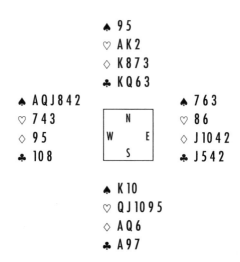

|  | ♠ 9 5 |  |
|---|---|---|
|  | ♡ A K 2 |  |
|  | ◇ K 8 7 3 |  |
|  | ♣ K Q 6 3 |  |
| ♠ A Q J 8 4 2 |  | ♠ 7 6 3 |
| ♡ 7 4 3 |  | ♡ 8 6 |
| ◇ 9 5 |  | ◇ J 10 4 2 |
| ♣ 10 8 |  | ♣ J 5 4 2 |
|  | ♠ K 10 |  |
|  | ♡ Q J 10 9 5 |  |
|  | ◇ A Q 6 |  |
|  | ♣ A 9 7 |  |

| WEST | NORTH | EAST | SOUTH |
|---|---|---|---|
| 2♠ | dbl | pass | 4NT |
| pass | 5◇ | pass | 6♡ |
| all pass |  |  |  |

South was tempted to bid 6♡ at his first turn. Playing with a partner who regards such leaps as uncultured, he inserted a Blackwood call on the way. How would you play the heart slam when West leads the ♡4?

You win the lead and draw trumps in two further rounds, noting that West began with three trumps. The most likely division of West's minor-suit cards is 2-2, in which case neither suit will yield an extra trick directly. A simple minor-suit squeeze on East is not possible, because he sits over the four-card holdings. (Also, you cannot safely concede a trick to rectify the count.)

You play your remaining two trumps, throwing two spades from dummy, and East has to discard all his spades in order to retain the two minor-suit guards. To investigate the lie of the minor suits, you continue with the ace and queen of diamonds, followed by the king and ace of clubs. West follows all the while, which gives him 6-3-2-2 shape. The ◇9 falls from West on the second round, but this does not help you, as East still holds the ◇J-10. Of more interest is the fall of the ♣10-8 from West. This leaves East with only ♣J-5, rendering him vulnerable to a throw-in.

These cards are left:

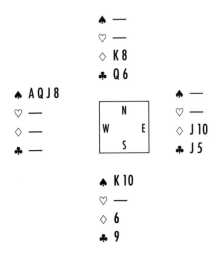

```
              ♠ —
              ♡ —
              ◇ K 8
              ♣ Q 6
  ♠ A Q J 8              ♠ —
  ♡ —          ┌─────┐   ♡ —
  ◇ —          │  N  │   ◇ J 10
  ♣ —        W │     │ E ♣ J 5
               │  S  │
               └─────┘
              ♠ K 10
              ♡ —
              ◇ 6
              ♣ 9
```

You cash the ◇K and put East on lead with the ◇8. On this trick you must discard the ♣9, which is blocking the path to dummy's ♣Q-6 tenace. East then has to lead from his ♣J-5 and you make the slam.

## UNBLOCKING TO PERMIT A REPEATED FINESSE

Sometimes you must unblock a card on the first round of the suit, so that the lead can subsequently be held in the opposite hand to repeat a finesse. Look at the diamond suit on this deal:

```
                        ♠ J 3 2
                        ♡ Q 6 4
                        ◇ K 8 7 2
                        ♣ Q 9 7
        ♠ 9                             ♠ K 8
        ♡ J 10 7 5 3     ┌─────────┐    ♡ K 9 8 2
        ◇ 10             │    N    │    ◇ Q 6 5 3
        ♣ K 10 8 6 5 4   │ W     E │    ♣ A J 3
                         │    S    │
                         └─────────┘
                        ♠ A Q 10 7 6 5 4
                        ♡ A
                        ◇ A J 9 4
                        ♣ 2
```

| WEST | NORTH | EAST | SOUTH |
|------|-------|------|-------|
|      |       | 1◇   | 1♠    |
| pass | 2♠    | pass | 4♣    |
| pass | 4◇    | pass | 6♠    |
| all pass |   |      |       |

No one at your club bids as wildly as that, I realize. Still, avert your eyes
politely from the bidding and see if you can make the contract. How will you
seek twelve tricks when West leads the ◇ 10?

You must win the opening lead with dummy's ◇ K, since you need to take
a trump finesse and there is no other entry to the table. Your labors on the first
trick are not yet over, however. You must also unblock the ◇ 9 from your hand
to facilitate taking diamond finesses later on.

You continue with a low trump to the queen, the defenders following with
low cards. You then draw the last trump with your ace and return to dummy
for the last time with the jack of trumps. 'Eight of diamonds, please,' you say.
East plays low and, thanks to your earlier unblock of the ◇ 9, you can under-
play with the ◇ 4 from your hand. Still in the dummy, you take a further diamond finesse and make the contract.

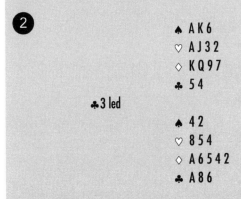

**1**

♠ A 2
♡ K 8 5
◇ A K 2
♣ 9 8 6 5 4

♠K led

♠ J 6 5 4
♡ A Q J 6 3
◇ —
♣ A K Q 10

With a reputation for aggressive bidding to uphold, you and your partner bid all the way to 7♡. How will you play the contract when West leads the ♠K? (Trumps will break 3-2.)

**2**

♠ A K 6
♡ A J 3 2
◇ K Q 9 7
♣ 5 4

♣3 led

♠ 4 2
♡ 8 5 4
◇ A 6 5 4 2
♣ A 8 6

| WEST | NORTH | EAST | SOUTH |
|------|-------|------|-------|
|  |  | 3♣ | pass |
| pass | dbl | pass | 3NT |
| all pass |  |  |  |

Showing due respect for his partner's preemptive opening, West leads the ♣3 against your 3NT contract. East plays the ♣9. What is your plan?

**3**

♠ K 8 5 3
♡ A K 10
◇ A K
♣ K 9 6 3

♡8 led

♠ A Q 10 7 6 4 2
♡ J 6
◇ 6 5
♣ 7 2

| WEST | NORTH | EAST | SOUTH |
|------|-------|------|-------|
|      |       | 1♡   | 3♠    |
| pass | 4NT   | pass | 5◇    |
| pass | 6♠    | all pass |    |

West leads the ♡8 against your small slam. How will you play the contract?

**4**

♠ A Q 8 7 4
♡ J 6 4
◇ 7 5 3
♣ J 7

◇8 led

♠ K 9 5
♡ K Q 3
◇ A K Q 4 2
♣ A 6

| WEST | NORTH | EAST | SOUTH |
|------|-------|------|-------|
|      |       |      | 2NT   |
| pass | 3♡    | pass | 4♠    |
| pass | 5♠    | pass | 6♠    |
| all pass |    |      |       |

West leads the ◇8 against your small slam, East playing the ◇6. How will you tackle the play?

**1**

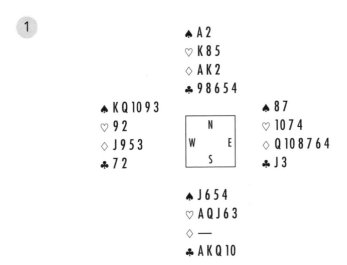

♠ A 2
♡ K 8 5
◇ A K 2
♣ 9 8 6 5 4

♠ K Q 10 9 3
♡ 9 2
◇ J 9 5 3
♣ 7 2

♠ 8 7
♡ 10 7 4
◇ Q 10 8 7 6 4
♣ J 3

♠ J 6 5 4
♡ A Q J 6 3
◇ —
♣ A K Q 10

West leads the ♠K against your grand slam in hearts. How will you play the contract?

Five hearts, five clubs and three top winners in the pointed suits will bring your total to thirteen. The only problem is… yes, that the club suit is blocked. With the ♠A removed by the opening lead, you will have to reach dummy's fifth club with the ♡K on the third round of trumps.

You win the spade lead and cash the ace and queen of trumps, pleased to see both defenders follow. Even though there is still a trump out, you must next cash the ace and king of clubs. When the cards lie as in the diagram, the suit will break 2-2. You cross to dummy with the ♡K, drawing East's last trump, and play the ◇A-K, throwing the two blocking clubs. The way is then clear for you to cash the ♣9-8-6, discarding the three spade losers from your hand.

You would also have made the contract when the defender with three trumps held ♣J-x-x or x-x-x. His partner would not be able to ruff the second round of clubs. You would continue with a third round of clubs from your hand to extract the jack (or the third spot). Then you would cross to the ♡K to discard your last club on the ◇A. Three discards would still be available for your spade losers — two on the clubs and one on the ◇K.

```
             ♠ A K 6
             ♡ A J 3 2
             ◇ K Q 9 7
             ♣ 5 4
♠ Q J 8 7 5              ♠ 10 9 3
♡ Q 10 7 6      N       ♡ K 9
◇ J 10 3     W     E    ◇ 8
♣ 3             S       ♣ K Q J 10 9 7 2
             ♠ 4 2
             ♡ 8 5 4
             ◇ A 6 5 4 2
             ♣ A 8 6
```

| WEST | NORTH | EAST | SOUTH |
|------|-------|------|-------|
|      |       | 3♣   | pass  |
| pass | dbl   | pass | 3NT   |
| all pass |   |      |       |

West leads the ♣3 against 3NT, East playing the ♣9. How will you play the contract?

Unless diamonds break 4-0, you have nine top tricks visible. If the defenders' diamonds break 3-1, however, the suit will be blocked. You will need to play the ace, king and queen to pick up the defenders' cards and the last spot card in dummy will then block the suit. How can you prevent this from happening?

Once you have spotted the problem, it is not too difficult to see the solution. You must discard the potentially blocking diamond on the third round of clubs. You allow East's ♣9 to win and he continues with the ♣K. Even though West has no more clubs, you must hold up the ♣A for a second time. When East persists with clubs, you win the third round with the ace and discard the ◇7 (or the ◇9) from dummy. The way is then clear for you to play the king, queen and another diamond, winning the third round with the ace. Since dummy has no diamond card remaining, you can score the ◇6 and the ◇5 at your leisure, giving you the contract.

If East were to switch to a spade at Trick 2, you would win and duck a second round of clubs yourself. As before, you would be able to discard a blocking diamond on the third round of clubs.

```
                      ♠ K 8 5 3
                      ♡ A K 10
                      ◇ A K
                      ♣ K 9 6 3
      ♠ 9                              ♠ J
      ♡ 8 7 4          ┌─────────┐     ♡ Q 9 5 3 2
      ◇ 9 8 4 3 2      │   N     │     ◇ Q J 10 7
      ♣ J 8 5 4        │ W     E │     ♣ A Q 10
                       │   S     │
                       └─────────┘
                      ♠ A Q 10 7 6 4 2
                      ♡ J 6
                      ◇ 6 5
                      ♣ 7 2
```

| WEST | NORTH | EAST | SOUTH |
|------|-------|------|-------|
|      |       | 1♡   | 3♠    |
| pass | 4NT   | pass | 5◇    |
| pass | 6♠    | all pass |   |

West leads the ♡8 against your small slam. How will you play the contract?

You have eleven tricks on top. There are only 13 points missing, so it is a near certainty that East holds the ♣A. The best chance is to catch him in a strip squeeze. You plan to reduce him to ♡Q-9 ♣A and then throw him in with a club to give you an extra heart trick.

Suppose you win the first trick with the ♡A and follow with the ♡6 from your hand. No throw-in play will be possible, because the ♡J will block the path into dummy's ♡K-10 tenace. You must therefore unblock the ♡J at Trick 1. After drawing trumps and cashing dummy's ◇A-K, you must continue to play all your trumps, reducing to ♡K-10 ♣K in the dummy. If you judge that East's last three cards are indeed the ♡Q-9 and the ♣A, you will throw East in with a club and he will have to return a heart into dummy's unfettered tenace.

If East attempts to fool you by baring the ♡Q and keeping ♣A-Q or ♣A-10, you will have to read the situation and drop his ♡Q. In such a situation, the cards played by West, the intended victim's partner, will often allow you to place the cards.

**4**

```
                    ♠ A Q 8 7 4
                    ♡ J 6 4
                    ◇ 7 5 3
                    ♣ J 7
    ♠ J 6 3 2                      ♠ 10
    ♡ 10 9 2          N           ♡ A 8 7 5
    ◇ 8          W         E      ◇ J 10 9 6
    ♣ K 10 8 5 4      S           ♣ Q 9 3 2
                    ♠ K 9 5
                    ♡ K Q 3
                    ◇ A K Q 4 2
                    ♣ A 6
```

| WEST | NORTH | EAST | SOUTH |
|------|-------|------|-------|
|      |       |      | 2NT   |
| pass | 3♡    | pass | 4♠    |
| pass | 5♠    | pass | 6♠    |
| all pass |    |      |       |

South breaks the transfer and North is encouraged to make a slam try, despite the two frail jacks in his hand. By this unconvincing route, South arrives in a small slam. How would you play this contract when West leads the ◇8 and East plays the ◇6?

You win the diamond lead in your hand and must now pick up the trumps. When East holds a singleton ♠10 or ♠J, a third-round finesse will be necessary. To prepare for this, you should lead the ♠9 to dummy's ♠A on the first round. Your diligence appears to have been rewarded when the ♠10 falls from East. You continue with a low trump to the king and then lead the ♠5 to dummy's ♠8, drawing West's last trump with the queen. (If you had not unblocked the ♠9, you would be stuck in the South hand when West refused to cover the nine on the third round.)

You now cash two more diamond winners, discovering that the opening lead was a singleton. You ruff a diamond in dummy, establishing the thirteenth card in the suit, and return to your hand with the ♣A. You can then knock out the ♡A to bring your total to twelve tricks. You make five trumps, four diamonds, two hearts and the ♣A. A club lead would have beaten the slam.

# CHAPTER 3

# UNUSUAL SUIT-ESTABLISHMENT TECHNIQUES

*Make it good*
A1

You may reckon there is little to be said about establishing a side suit. 'Ruff a round or two and see if the suit breaks favorably, man. That's all there is to it.' Think again! There are various interesting techniques that can assist you in the process and this chapter will present the most important of them.

## LEAVE THE LAST ROUND OF TRUMPS AS AN ENTRY

Suppose your trump holding is K-x-x in the dummy opposite A-Q-x-x-x in your hand. When you are short of entries to the dummy, it may suit you to draw only two rounds of trumps, with the ace and the queen, and then to leave one trump outstanding while you establish dummy's long suit. It is a familiar technique and sometimes you must risk an adverse ruff while employing it:

```
                    ♠ K 6 4
                    ♡ 9 7 5
                    ◇ 5 2
                    ♣ Q 10 8 7 4
    ♠ 10 8 2                        ♠ 9 7
    ♡ Q J 4         ┌─────────┐     ♡ K 10 8 2
    ◇ K J 9 3       │    N    │     ◇ Q 10 8 7 4
    ♣ A 9 2         │ W     E │     ♣ 5 3
                    │    S    │
                    └─────────┘
                    ♠ A Q J 5 3
                    ♡ A 6 3
                    ◇ A 6
                    ♣ K J 6
```

| WEST | NORTH | EAST | SOUTH |
|------|-------|------|-------|
|      |       |      | 1♠ |
| pass | 2♠ | pass | 4♠ |
| all pass |  |  |  |

West finds the threatening heart lead, placing the ♡Q on the table. What now?

You might as well duck the first trick. You win the heart continuation (or diamond switch) and draw two rounds of trumps with the ace and the queen. Even though a club ruff will now sink the contract, you must risk playing on clubs. Here, fortunately, the defender with the doubleton club has no trumps left, so the defenders cannot score a club ruff. When you regain the lead you will cross to the ♠K, drawing West's last trump, and discard a red-suit loser on dummy's clubs.

Here is a more complex example of this style of play, where declarer caters for adverse breaks of the side suit he needs to establish.

```
                      ♠ 10 5
                      ♡ Q 10 9 6 4
                      ◇ 7 5 3
                      ♣ K 8 3
     ♠ K J 9 7 6 4 2              ♠ Q 8 3
     ♡ 2              ┌─────────┐   ♡ J 8 5 3
     ◇ Q J 6 4        │ N       │   ◇ K 9 2
     ♣ 5              │ W     E │   ♣ J 10 4
                      │    S    │
                      └─────────┘
                      ♠ A
                      ♡ A K 7
                      ◇ A 10 8
                      ♣ A Q 9 7 6 2
```

| WEST | NORTH | EAST | SOUTH |
|------|-------|------|-------|
|      |       |      | 1♣    |
| 1♠   | 2♣    | 2♠   | 6♣    |
| all pass |    |      |       |

Well, like it or not, that's the way the bidding went. How would you play
the small slam when West leads the ♠7 and East plays the ♠Q?

After winning the spade lead, you should draw two rounds of trumps with
the ace and queen. When the 3-1 break comes to light, you should continue
with the ace and king of hearts. Suppose East started with a singleton heart and
ruffs the second round. This will cause no problem because you will be able to
finesse the ♡10 on the third round. If instead the hearts break 3-2, you will
simply draw the last trump before continuing hearts. When the cards lie as in
the diagram, West shows out on the second heart. You cross to the heart queen
and ruff a heart. You can then return to dummy with the trump king to enjoy
the long heart, discarding one of your diamond losers.

If West had found the more taxing lead of a diamond, you might well play
the contract the same way. You would have to judge, on the evidence available,
whether East or West was more likely to hold a singleton heart.

## ESTABLISHING THE SUIT WITH A HIGH RUFF

Sometimes it pays to establish the main side suit with a high ruff, even if this sets up an extra trump trick for the defenders. Look at this deal:

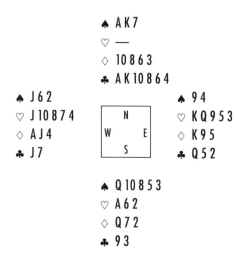

&spades; A K 7
&hearts; —
&diams; 10 8 6 3
&clubs; A K 10 8 6 4

&spades; J 6 2
&hearts; J 10 8 7 4
&diams; A J 4
&clubs; J 7

&spades; 9 4
&hearts; K Q 9 5 3
&diams; K 9 5
&clubs; Q 5 2

&spades; Q 10 8 5 3
&hearts; A 6 2
&diams; Q 7 2
&clubs; 9 3

| WEST | NORTH | EAST | SOUTH |
|------|-------|------|-------|
| | 1&clubs; | 1&hearts; | 1&spades; |
| 3&hearts; | 3&spades; | pass | 4&spades; |
| all pass | | | |

West leads the &hearts;J against your spade game. How will you play the contract?

The original declarer threw a diamond from dummy and won with the &hearts;A. He then played a trump to the ace and continued with dummy's two top club honors. Both defenders followed politely and he continued with a third round of clubs, not overjoyed to see East produce the last club. What now?

Declarer tried his luck with the &spades;10. Not the best! West overruffed with the &spades;J and was not pressed to switch to the &diams;4. The defenders pocketed three diamond tricks and that was down one.

Declarer's line of play might have been assessed as a calculated gamble at matchpoints. Playing IMPs, it was rather careless. He should have ruffed with the &spades;Q, avoiding any risk of an overruff. He could then draw a second round of trumps with dummy's &spades;K and play a good club, discarding a diamond. Even though West could ruff this trick, the defenders would score just one trump and two diamonds.

## DUCKING THE FIRST ROUND TO PREVENT A HOLD-UP

When you are playing in notrump with ◊A-K-x-x-x-x in the dummy and ◊x-x in your hand, it is a familiar play to duck the first round. You will have to lose at least one trick in the suit anyway. After ducking the first round, you can cross to dummy on the second round and perhaps then run the suit.

The same first-round ducking play can pay off with other honor holdings in the dummy. Look at the club suit here:

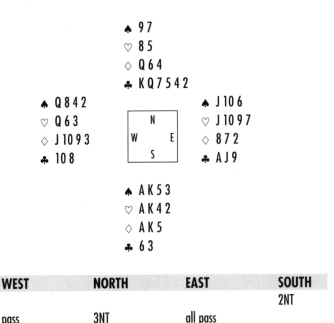

```
                    ♠ 9 7
                    ♡ 8 5
                    ◊ Q 6 4
                    ♣ K Q 7 5 4 2
    ♠ Q 8 4 2                      ♠ J 10 6
    ♡ Q 6 3          N             ♡ J 10 9 7
    ◊ J 10 9 3    W     E          ◊ 8 7 2
    ♣ 10 8           S             ♣ A J 9
                    ♠ A K 5 3
                    ♡ A K 4 2
                    ◊ A K 5
                    ♣ 6 3
```

| WEST | NORTH | EAST | SOUTH |
|------|-------|------|-------|
|      |       |      | 2NT   |
| pass | 3NT   | all pass |    |

West led the ◊J and the original declarer won with the ace, continuing with a club to the king. If East had captured with the ace, the contract would easily have been made. Declarer could win the diamond return with the king, cross to the ♣Q and clear the club suit. The ◊Q would remain as an entry to the established winners in clubs. However, Easy was alert to the situation and allowed the ♣K to win. The contract could no longer be made. Declarer returned to his hand and led to the ♣Q but this lost to East's ace and the club suit was dead.

To prevent this hold-up by East, you must duck the first round of clubs completely. Whichever defender happens to win the first round of clubs, you will win the diamond continuation with the king and play a club to the king. It will do East no good to hold up now because the lead is in dummy! You will be able to clear the club suit. Whether East chooses to win the second or the third round of clubs, the suit will be established and you will make game.

It was right to play clubs in this way because you could afford to lose two clubs and two spades. On many deals you could not afford the loss of two club tricks. You would then have to lead to the ♣K on the first round, hoping to find West with ♣A-x or ♣A-x-x.

The same play can be effective when dummy's only honor in the long suit is the king. Again you may need to duck the first round.

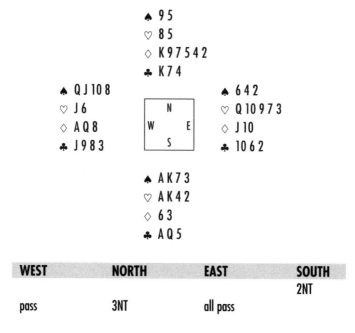

| WEST | NORTH | EAST | SOUTH |
|------|-------|------|-------|
|      |       |      | 2NT   |
| pass | 3NT   | all pass |    |

West leads the ♠Q against 3NT. You win with the ♠A and see that you must set up dummy's diamond suit. You will need to find the ◇A onside, in which case you hope to lose just two spades and two diamonds. Suppose your first move is to play a diamond to the king, winning the trick. You will go down! The defenders will win the second round of diamonds and, with only one entry left to the dummy, you will have no chance to establish and enjoy the diamond suit.

As on the previous deal, you must duck the first round of diamonds. East wins and returns a spade. You win with the ♠K and play a diamond to the queen and king. That's better! By following this line, you use the ◇K as an entry on the second round (rather than the first), which allows you to play a third round of diamonds, setting up the suit. West wins with the ◇A and cashes. two spade winners, but the remaining tricks are yours.

## Playing for the last trump to lie well

Sometimes the side suit that you wish to establish lies in declarer's hand, alongside the long trumps. Suppose you have a side suit of K-Q-8-7-4 in your hand opposite A-6-2 in the dummy. If you can draw trumps and still have a trump left in dummy, a 4-1 break in the side suit will not inconvenience you. You can establish the suit by ruffing the fourth round of the suit. Even when there is still a trump out, you may be able to establish the suit with a ruff. All will depend on which defender holds the last trump.

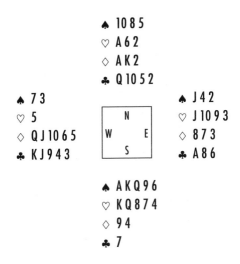

```
            ♠ 10 8 5
            ♡ A 6 2
            ◇ A K 2
            ♣ Q 10 5 2
♠ 7 3                        ♠ J 4 2
♡ 5            N            ♡ J 10 9 3
◇ Q J 10 6 5   W    E       ◇ 8 7 3
♣ K J 9 4 3        S        ♣ A 8 6
            ♠ A K Q 9 6
            ♡ K Q 8 7 4
            ◇ 9 4
            ♣ 7
```

| WEST | NORTH | EAST | SOUTH |
|------|-------|------|-------|
|  | 1♣ | pass | 1♠ |
| pass | 1NT | pass | 3♡ |
| pass | 3♠ | pass | 4♣ |
| pass | 4◇ | pass | 4NT |
| pass | 5♡ | pass | 6♠ |
| all pass | | | |

How would you play the slam when West leads the ◇ Q, won in dummy?

If you draw all the trumps, you will need the heart suit to divide 3-2. A better idea is to draw just two rounds of trumps and then play the ace and king of hearts. If hearts do break 3-2, you simply draw the last trump and score twelve top tricks. When hearts are 4-1, you give yourself the extra chance that the last trump may lie with the heart length. You play your third top heart, ruff a heart in dummy (East following impotently) and concede a club trick. Eventually, you will return to your hand with a club ruff and draw East's last trump.

Here is a more complex deal on the same theme:

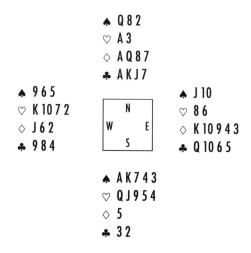

```
              ♠ Q 8 2
              ♡ A 3
              ◇ A Q 8 7
              ♣ A K J 7
♠ 9 6 5                       ♠ J 10
♡ K 10 7 2        N           ♡ 8 6
◇ J 6 2      W         E      ◇ K 10 9 4 3
♣ 9 8 4           S           ♣ Q 10 6 5
              ♠ A K 7 4 3
              ♡ Q J 9 5 4
              ◇ 5
              ♣ 3 2
```

| WEST | NORTH | EAST | SOUTH |
|------|-------|------|-------|
|      | 2NT   | pass | 3♠    |
| pass | 4♣    | pass | 4NT   |
| pass | 5♣    | pass | 6♠    |
| all pass |    |      |       |

How will you play the spade slam when West leads the ♠5?

You need to set up the heart suit. If you draw all the trumps and play ace and another heart, you will go down when the hearts lie as in the diagram. You can improve your chances by drawing just two rounds of trumps and then attempting to ruff a heart. It is not easy to time the play correctly. Suppose you win the trump lead with the ace. If you play ace and another heart now, West will return a third round of hearts, promoting a trump trick for the defenders.

If instead you play the ace and queen of trumps before playing ace and another heart, West will remove dummy's last trump when he wins with the heart king. What can be done?

You should win the trump lead with dummy's queen and play a low heart from dummy. West wins the queen with the king and plays a second round of trumps to your ace. Both defenders follow to the ace of hearts and you reach your hand by cashing the ◇A and ruffing a diamond. You then ruff a heart with dummy's last trump. This is safe when hearts were 3-3 all along. It gains heavily when East has only two hearts but does not hold the last trump. You will return to your hand with another diamond ruff, draw West's last trump and triumphantly claim twelve tricks.

## FORCING THE DEFENDERS TO PLAY THE LONG SUIT

Sometimes the entries to dummy are insufficient to establish a side suit and to reach the long cards. In that case, you may be able to force the defenders to play a round of the suit for you. That's what happens on this deal:

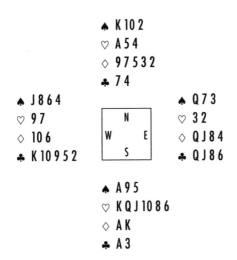

| WEST | NORTH | EAST | SOUTH |
|------|-------|------|-------|
| | | | 1♡ |
| pass | 2♡ | pass | 2♠ |
| pass | 4♡ | pass | 6♡ |
| all pass | | | |

You follow an eccentric sequence to a small slam in hearts and West leads the ♡7. How will you play the contract?

You would like to set up dummy's diamond suit, but the cruel disposition of the trump spot cards means that there are only two entries to dummy. If diamonds break 3-3, all will be well. You can use one entry to set up the diamonds with a ruff and then use the second entry to reach the long cards. What if the diamond suit breaks 4-2? Is there any chance then?

You win the trump lead in your hand and draw a second round of trumps with the king, both defenders following. You then cash the ace and king of diamonds. Suppose your next move is to cross to dummy and ruff a diamond. No good! West will show out on the third round of diamonds and there will be no way to recover.

After cashing the top diamonds, the winning line is to play ace and another club. The defender who wins the trick will not relish the moment. He cannot play a club, because this would give you a ruff-and-sluff. Nor can he safely play a spade, because you would then make the contract by playing for the queen and jack to lie in different hands. The only other possibility is that East wins the second club and plays a diamond. But, of course, this will assist you in establishing the diamond suit. You will ruff in your hand, cross to dummy and ruff a fourth round of diamonds. One entry to dummy remains to enjoy the established long diamond, on which you will discard a spade from your hand.

## Avoiding a trump promotion

When you must rely on a trump entry and therefore cannot draw trumps at the start of the deal, you may need to take precautions to avoid suffering an over-ruff or trump promotion in the key suit. This deal illustrates the problem:

                    ♠ A 8 2
                    ♡ K 7 6
                    ◇ Q 5
                    ♣ J 9 6 5 2

    ♠ Q 10                         ♠ J 5
    ♡ Q 9 4 2         N            ♡ J 10 5
    ◇ J 10 9 3 2    W   E          ◇ 8 7 6 4
    ♣ 7 3              S           ♣ K Q 10 8

                    ♠ K 9 7 6 4 3
                    ♡ A 8 3
                    ◇ A K
                    ♣ A 4

| WEST | NORTH | EAST | SOUTH |
|------|-------|------|-------|
|      |       |      | 1♠    |
| pass | 3♠    | pass | 6♠    |
| all pass |   |      |       |

You and your partner would have bid the hands differently, I realize. Still, treat it as a play problem. West leads the ◇J against the spade slam. How will you organize the play?

You will need a 2-2 trump break and must aim to set up dummy's club suit, so that you can discard your heart loser. Entries to dummy are not plentiful and if you open the proceedings by cashing the top two trumps, you will need the clubs to break 3-3. How can you make the slam when clubs are 4-2?

After winning the diamond lead, you should play the ♣4 from your hand! You can see what would happen if you played ace and another club instead.

East would win and play a third round of clubs to promote a trump trick for the defense. After your safer play of a low club, East wins and switches to the ♡J. You win with the ♡A and draw one round of trumps with the king. You then unblock the ♣A and cross to dummy with the ♠A, nodding approvingly at the 2-2 trump break. You still have two entries to the dummy (the ♠8 and the ♡K) so it is a simple matter to establish the thirteenth club and return to dummy to discard your heart loser on it.

Suppose you had drawn one round of trumps with the king before ducking the first round of clubs. No good. East can then remove the ♠A entry to dummy with a trump return. For the same reason, the opening lead of a trump (unlikely) or a heart would have broken the slam. East would again be able to remove one of dummy's entry when he won the first round of clubs.

## DELIBERATELY LOSING TRUMP CONTROL

We will end the chapter with a somewhat strange deal on which many declarers would tumble to defeat. See how you do.

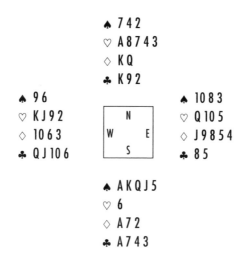

|       | ♠ 7 4 2        |       |        |
|       | ♡ A 8 7 4 3    |       |        |
|       | ◇ K Q          |       |        |
|       | ♣ K 9 2        |       |        |

| ♠ 9 6 | | ♠ 10 8 3 |
| ♡ K J 9 2 | | ♡ Q 10 5 |
| ◇ 10 6 3 | | ◇ J 9 8 5 4 |
| ♣ Q J 10 6 | | ♣ 8 5 |

|       | ♠ A K Q J 5    |       |        |
|       | ♡ 6            |       |        |
|       | ◇ A 7 2        |       |        |
|       | ♣ A 7 4 3      |       |        |

| WEST | NORTH | EAST | SOUTH |
| --- | --- | --- | --- |
|  | 1♡ | pass | 1♠ |
| pass | 2♠ | pass | 6♠ |
| all pass |  |  |  |

West leads the ♣Q against your spade slam. What is your plan for twelve tricks?

A 3-3 club break is less likely than normal, since West's ♣Q opening lead suggests a sequence and at least a four-card suit. One possible line is to duck a round of clubs, aiming to draw two rounds of trumps and ruff the fourth round of clubs if necessary. This would fail here. Instead, you should aim to set up a long card in hearts. The first move is obvious. You win the opening lead with the ♣A, preserving the entries to the hand containing the long side suit. What next?

Suppose you draw three rounds of trumps, planning to ruff two hearts and duck one heart thereafter. You will cross to the ♡A and ruff one heart, return to the ◇K and ruff another heart. You can then return to dummy with the ◇Q to duck a round of hearts and the ♣K will remain in dummy to reach the established long heart. Yes, but you will never score a trick with the ◇A!

Let's try something different. You draw just two rounds of trumps and then play to ruff three hearts in your hand. Ace of hearts, heart ruff, ◇K, heart ruff. You then cross to the ◇Q and take a third heart ruff with your last trump. East takes the opportunity to throw his last club on this trick and these cards remain:

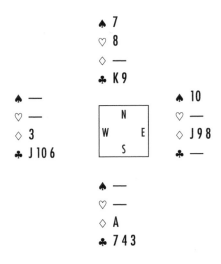

You cash the ◇A, throwing the ♣9 from dummy, and play a club to the king. East is welcome to ruff, because you will ruff his diamond return and, at last, enjoy the ♡8.

What is the lesson from this deal? When the entry situation may become difficult, make sure that you check your line of play all the way through to its successful conclusion.

**1**

♠ 9 7 4
♡ 7 4
◇ K 8 3
♣ Q 7 6 5 2

♡K led

♠ A K Q J 2
♡ A 6
◇ A J 5 4 2
♣ A

| WEST | NORTH | EAST | SOUTH |
|------|-------|------|-------|
|      |       |      | 2♣    |
| 2♡   | pass  | pass | 2♠    |
| pass | 4♠    | pass | 5♣    |
| pass | 5◇    | pass | 6♠    |
| all pass |   |      |       |

How will you play the spade slam when West leads the ♡K?

**2**

♠ 8 4 3
♡ A 4
◇ 5 4 3
♣ A Q 7 6 4

◇J led

♠ A K Q J 7
♡ K 7
◇ A K 6 2
♣ 9 3

| WEST | NORTH | EAST | SOUTH |
|------|-------|------|-------|
|      |       |      | 1♠    |
| pass | 2♣    | pass | 2◇    |
| pass | 3♠    | pass | 4NT   |
| pass | 5♡    | pass | 6♠    |
| all pass |   |      |       |

West leads the ◇J against 6♠. What's your best chance for the contract?

1

```
            ♠ 9 7 4
            ♡ 7 4
            ◇ K 8 3
            ♣ Q 7 6 5 2
♠ 8 3                        ♠ 10 6 5
♡ K Q J 10 3 2    N         ♡ 9 8 5
◇ 10          W       E     ◇ Q 9 7 6
♣ J 9 4 3         S         ♣ K 10 8
            ♠ A K Q J 2
            ♡ A 6
            ◇ A J 5 4 2
            ♣ A
```

| WEST | NORTH | EAST | SOUTH |
|------|-------|------|-------|
|      |       |      | 2♣ |
| 2♡ | pass | pass | 2♠ |
| pass | 4♠ | pass | 5♣ |
| pass | 5◇ | pass | 6♠ |
| all pass | | | |

North shows a useful card or two with his leap to 4♠. The double raise is non-forcing, of course; he would make the stronger bid of 3♠ if his hand were any stronger. You suggest a slam with a cuebid in clubs and North is happy to cuebid the ◇K. How would you tackle the resultant contract of 6♠ when West leads the ♡K?

You win the heart lead and play the ace and king of trumps, both defenders following. If you draw the last trump next, you will need a 3-2 diamond break, as well as to find East with the ◇Q. A better idea is to leave the last trump outstanding while you take a look at the diamond suit. You cross to the ◇K and finesse the ◇J. The finesse wins and West shows out, discarding a heart. Since you still have a trump in dummy, the 4-1 diamond break presents no problem. You continue with the ace of diamonds and ruff a fourth round of the suit. You can then return to your hand with the ♣A to draw East's last trump and claim the contract.

```
                        ♠ 8 4 3
                        ♡ A 4
                        ◇ 5 4 3
                        ♣ A Q 7 6 4
     ♠ 10 6                              ♠ 9 5 2
     ♡ J 8 6 5 3        ┌─────────┐      ♡ Q 10 9 2
     ◇ J 10 9 7         │    N    │      ◇ Q 8
     ♣ K 8            W │         │ E    ♣ J 10 5 2
                        │    S    │
                        └─────────┘
                        ♠ A K Q J 7
                        ♡ K 7
                        ◇ A K 6 2
                        ♣ 9 3
```

| WEST | NORTH | EAST | SOUTH |
|------|-------|------|-------|
|  |  |  | 1♠ |
| pass | 2♣ | pass | 2◇ |
| pass | 3♠ | pass | 4NT |
| pass | 5♡ | pass | 6♠ |
| all pass |  |  |  |

West leads the ◇J against your small slam in spades. How will you give the contract the best chance?

Suppose you begin by ducking a diamond trick. You will then lose only one diamond trick when the suit breaks 3-3 or when you can successfully ruff the fourth round in dummy. However, you will still need to find the ♣K onside. That being so, it is much better to rely on establishing the club suit for a diamond discard.

You win the diamond lead and draw trumps in three rounds. If you continue with a club to the queen, you will need the clubs to break 3-3 (or, as a fall-back, the diamonds to be 3-3). A better idea is to duck a round of clubs, planning to finesse the ♣Q on the second round. You win the red-suit return in your hand and lead another club. When the cards lie as in the diagram, the ♣K will appear and you win with the ♣A. You then cash the ♣Q and ruff the fourth round of clubs. The ♡A remains as an entry to the long club.

As it happens, a heart lead ('Lead the unbid suit, partner!') would have beaten the contract, because the defenders could kill the heart entry to dummy if a round of clubs was ducked.

# CHAPTER 4

# PROTECT YOUR HONORS FROM GETTING RUFFED

*Protect me*
Placebo

Various techniques are available to prevent your honors from getting ruffed. We will see the best of them in this chapter.

## PROTECT YOUR HONORS BY WINNING IN THE RIGHT HAND

One of the simplest ways to prevent an honor being ruffed involves merely winning the opening lead in the right hand. Look at this deal:

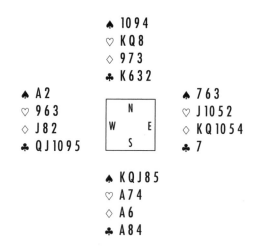

```
            ♠ 10 9 4
            ♡ K Q 8
            ◇ 9 7 3
            ♣ K 6 3 2
♠ A 2                        ♠ 7 6 3
♡ 9 6 3           N          ♡ J 10 5 2
◇ J 8 2       W       E      ◇ K Q 10 5 4
♣ Q J 10 9 5      S          ♣ 7
            ♠ K Q J 8 5
            ♡ A 7 4
            ◇ A 6
            ♣ A 8 4
```

| WEST | NORTH | EAST | SOUTH |
|------|-------|------|-------|
|  |  |  | 1♠ |
| pass | 2♠ | pass | 4♠ |
| all pass |  |  |  |

West leads the ♣Q against your spade game. How will you play?

Suppose you win the club lead with the ace and play a trump. When West takes the ace, he will persevere with the ♣J and East will be able to ruff dummy's ♣K. Down one!

To make sure that East does not have a chance to ruff a club honor, you must win the first trick with dummy's ♣K. You play trumps, as before, but now a second round of clubs from West does not hurt you. If East ruffs, he will be ruffing a loser. Your ♣A will live to fight another day.

Why was it right to win the opening lead with dummy's king? Because the opening lead of the ♣Q was much more likely to be from a sequence than a singleton. If anyone held a singleton club, which was the main risk to the contract, it was likely to be East. Suppose instead that West had led a spot card such as the ♣9 or the ♣7. The odds would then switch. East would be more likely to hold five clubs and you would therefore win the opening lead with the ♣A. If East did hold ♣Q-J-10-x-x and the trump ace, he would not benefit by continuing clubs when he gained the lead. West would be ruffing a loser.

## PROTECT YOUR HONORS BY LEADING TOWARDS THEM

Another very common technique is to lead towards your side-suit honors, through the defender who is in a position to ruff. Consequently, he can ruff only the low card that you have led and not an honor. You should play that way on a deal like this:

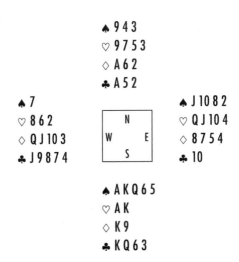

```
               ♠ 9 4 3
               ♡ 9 7 5 3
               ◇ A 6 2
               ♣ A 5 2
 ♠ 7                          ♠ J 10 8 2
 ♡ 8 6 2          N           ♡ Q J 10 4
 ◇ Q J 10 3   W     E         ◇ 8 7 5 4
 ♣ J 9 8 7 4      S           ♣ 10
               ♠ A K Q 6 5
               ♡ A K
               ◇ K 9
               ♣ K Q 6 3
```

| WEST | NORTH | EAST | SOUTH |
|------|-------|------|-------|
|  |  |  | 2♣ |
| pass | 2◇ | pass | 2♠ |
| pass | 3♠ | pass | 4NT |
| pass | 5♡ | pass | 6♠ |
| all pass |  |  |  |

If North had held four-card spade support, a grand slam would be worth bidding. You take a conservative view (for a change) and stop in a small slam. How will you play the contract when West leads the ◇Q?

You should win with the ◇K, preserving the two entries to dummy. All will be well if trumps are 3-2, so you start by drawing two rounds of trumps. West shows out on the second round of trumps, discarding a heart. What now?

You must make arrangements for your fourth club. The card can be ruffed in dummy, provided that you can score your three club honors without one of them being ruffed by a defender. East will have to follow to one round of clubs, but that is all you require, as long as you play the contract properly.

After the second round of trumps, play a club to the ace, East following. When you lead a second round of clubs towards the honors in your hand, East will gain nothing by ruffing a losing club with his master trump. He discards instead and you win with the ♣K. You re-enter dummy with the ◇A and lead a third round of clubs towards your hand. Again East cannot gain by ruffing. He discards and you win with the ♣Q. You still have two black-suit losers in your hand, but they are about to be merged into one. You ruff your last club with dummy's ♠9 and it makes no difference whether East decides to overruff or not. He will score a trump trick at some stage and the remaining tricks are yours.

If you had carelessly won the opening lead in the dummy, you would have gone down. With East holding only one club, you needed two entries to dummy, so that you could lead twice towards the club honors in your hand.

Next we will see a deal where you need to establish a suit in which one of the defenders holds a singleton. By leading towards the honors, you not only save them from being ruffed, you are also able to establish the suit.

```
                    ♠ —
                    ♡ Q 7 5 3
                    ♦ A Q J 5
                    ♣ A K Q 5 2
   ♠ J 10 7 3                      ♠ 2
   ♡ K J 8 2          ┌─────────┐  ♡ A 10 9 6 4
   ♦ 10 8 4 3      W  │    N    │E  ♦ K 7 6
   ♣ 3                │    S    │   ♣ J 10 7 4
                      └─────────┘
                    ♠ A K Q 9 8 6 5 4
                    ♡ —
                    ♦ 9 2
                    ♣ 9 8 6
```

| WEST | NORTH | EAST | SOUTH |
|------|-------|------|-------|
|      | 1♣    | pass | 1♠    |
| pass | 2♦    | pass | 3♠    |
| pass | 3NT   | pass | 6♠    |
| all pass |   |      |       |

A diamond lead would have worked well, as it happens, but West decides
to lead the ♣3 against your spade slam. How will you play the contract?

You win with the ♣A and reach your hand with a heart ruff. When you
play the ace and king of trumps, East shows out on the second round. You now
have a loser in the trump suit. To avoid relying on the diamond finesse, you will
need to discard a diamond loser on dummy's clubs. How can you manage that
in the dangerous case where West's club lead was a singleton?

You draw a third round of trumps and lead a club towards dummy's
remaining honors. It will do West no good to ruff a loser, since dummy's clubs
will then be established. Let's assume that he discards instead and you win the
trick with dummy's ♣K. You return to your hand with a heart ruff (you didn't
throw all dummy's hearts on the trumps, did you?) and lead another round of
clubs towards dummy. Once more, West cannot profitably ruff in the second
seat. You win with the ♣Q and ruff a club, setting up a long card in the suit.
If West overruffs, dummy's ♦A will be an entry to the long club. If West
declines to overruff, you can give him his trump trick and again take a discard
on the long club.

Note how important it was to lead towards dummy on the second and third round of clubs. If West had been allowed to ruff a club honor, the slam would have gone down.

## CASH YOUR WINNERS BEFORE THEY CAN BE RUFFED

Another important technique is to cash your winners before the defenders can take a discard in the suit. This is common knowledge on crossruff deals. The same idea can apply even when you are taking a single ruff in the short-trump hand.

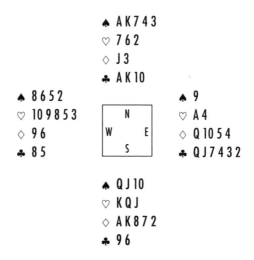

| WEST | NORTH | EAST | SOUTH |
|------|-------|------|-------|
| | | | 1NT |
| pass | 2♡ | pass | 2♠ |
| pass | 4NT | pass | 6♠ |
| all pass | | | |

North's 4NT is invitational and you judge that your hand is worth a small slam in spades. How will you play this contract when West leads the ♡10 to East's ace and the ♡4 is returned?

You have eleven top tricks and a club ruff in the short-trump hand (South) will provide an easy twelfth. You win the second round of hearts and draw two rounds of trumps with the queen and the jack, East throwing a club on the second round. What now? If you take your club ruff immediately, you will regret it. When you ruff the third round of clubs with the ♠10, West will discard one of his diamonds. The only route back to the North hand to draw the last trump is to cash two top diamonds and then ruff a diamond. Unfortunately, West will ruff the second diamond and you will be down one.

To avoid a diamond honor being ruffed, you must cash the ace-king of diamonds before playing for a club ruff. That's all there is to it. After taking the club ruff, you can return to dummy with a diamond ruff to draw West's last trump.

## DUCK A ROUND TO PREVENT AN HONOR BEING RUFFED

Finally, you can avoid an honor being ruffed by refusing to play it when there is a chance that it will be ruffed. You duck a round instead, ruff a further loser in the suit and then draw trumps. That is the winning line on this deal, where many players would go down.

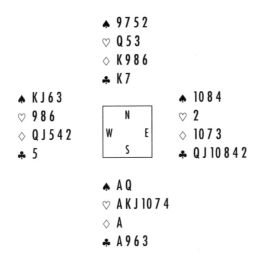

| WEST | NORTH | EAST | SOUTH |
|------|-------|------|-------|
|  |  |  | 2♣ |
| pass | 2♢ | pass | 2♡ |
| pass | 3♡ | pass | 3♠ |
| pass | 4♣ | pass | 6♡ |
| all pass |  |  |  |

With 7 points in his own hand, West knew that his partner was unlikely to hold an ace. Rather than lead his singleton club, he found the stronger lead of a trump. Pick up the South cards now. How will you play the contract when the ♡6 is led and East follows with the ♡2?

The original declarer played with commendable speed, but insufficient skill. After winning the trump lead, he cashed the ◊A and crossed to dummy with the ♣K. He discarded his potential spade loser on the ◊K and continued blithely with a club to the ace. Disaster! West ruffed and returned another trump. Dummy then held only one trump and declarer needed to ruff two losing clubs. No recovery was possible and the slam went down one.

Declarer failed to count his tricks. Six trump tricks, five side-suit winners and one club ruff would bring the total to twelve. The only real threat to the contract was that a club honor would be ruffed. Declarer should have ducked the second round of clubs. Even if West ruffs his partner's winning club and plays another trump, nothing can prevent declarer from ruffing his remaining loser in clubs. The ♣A can be banked safely after trumps have been drawn.

**1**

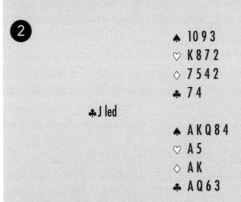

♠ A Q 7
♡ Q J 10 5
◇ 10 9 8 5
♣ A 9

♣K led

♠ K 3
♡ A K 4 3
◇ A K 7 6 3
♣ 10 5

| WEST | NORTH | EAST | SOUTH |
|------|-------|------|-------|
|      |       |      | 1◇    |
| 2♣   | dbl   | pass | 4♡    |
| pass | 4NT   | pass | 5♣    |
| pass | 6♡    | all pass |   |

West leads the ♣K and you win with dummy's ♣A. When you play the ace and queen of trumps, West discards a club on the second round. How will you continue?

**2**

♠ 10 9 3
♡ K 8 7 2
◇ 7 5 4 2
♣ 7 4

♣J led

♠ A K Q 8 4
♡ A 5
◇ A K
♣ A Q 6 3

You arrive in 6♠ and West leads the ♣J, East playing the ♣K. How will you play the hand?

1

```
              ♠ A Q 7
              ♡ Q J 10 5
              ◇ 10 9 8 5
              ♣ A 9
♠ J 10 5                        ♠ 9 8 6 4 2
♡ 7           ┌─────────┐       ♡ 9 8 6 2
◇ Q J 4       │ W  N  E │       ◇ 2
♣ K Q J 7 4 3 │    S    │       ♣ 8 6 2
              └─────────┘
              ♠ K 3
              ♡ A K 4 3
              ◇ A K 7 6 3
              ♣ 10 5
```

| WEST | NORTH | EAST | SOUTH |
|------|-------|------|-------|
|      |       |      | 1◇ |
| 2♣ | dbl | pass | 4♡ |
| pass | 4NT | pass | 5♣ |
| pass | 6♡ | all pass | |

West leads the ♣K and you win with dummy's ♣A. When you play the ace and queen of trumps, West discards a club on the second round. How will you continue?

Obviously you cannot afford to draw all the trumps before setting up the diamond suit. Nor can you afford to get one of your diamond honors ruffed, should East hold a singleton in the suit. You play a diamond to the ace and then cash the king, ace and queen of spades, throwing your club loser. Conveniently in the dummy, you now lead a second round of diamonds towards your remaining honor in the suit.

What can East do? If he ruffs, it will be the last trick for his side. You will win his return, draw trumps and enjoy the rest of the diamond suit. Let's suppose that East discards a club instead. You will win with the ◇K and concede a diamond trick to West. When West continues with a high club, you can ruff in your hand with the ♡K and lead the ♡4 to dummy's ♡J, proceeding to draw East's last trump. At Trick 13, you score a good diamond in the dummy.

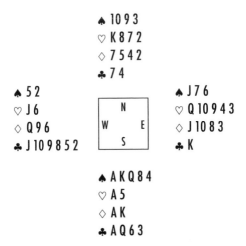

② ♠ 10 9 3
♡ K 8 7 2
◇ 7 5 4 2
♣ 7 4

♠ 5 2
♡ J 6
◇ Q 9 6
♣ J 10 9 8 5 2

♠ J 7 6
♡ Q 10 9 4 3
◇ J 10 8 3
♣ K

♠ A K Q 8 4
♡ A 5
◇ A K
♣ A Q 6 3

You bid to a small slam in spades and appear to be off to a good start when West leads the ♣J. East plays the ♣K and you win with the ♣A. How should you continue?

It looks almost too easy. You can cash the ♣Q and ruff a club with the ♠10. Even if East began with only two clubs and overruffs with the ♠J, you will still be able to ruff your last club loser with dummy's ♠9. What could possibly go wrong?

The answer is that East's ♣K might be a singleton. In that case, he will ruff the ♣Q with a low trump and may still be able to score an overruff with the ♠J later. Don't think to yourself, 'A 6-1 club break is not very likely.' Such breaks become much more likely when an honor is led, suggesting that the leader holds a longish suit headed by a sequence. Also, East would not generally play the ♣K unless he had to, because West would not lead away from the ♣A. South is therefore marked with the ♣A-Q. Anyway, what can you do to guard against the situation where clubs do break 6-1?

Yes, you must lead towards the ♣Q. So, cross to the ♡K at Trick 2 and lead a club towards your hand. If East follows suit, or discards, you will win with the club queen and ruff a club with the ♠10. It will not matter if East overruffs, since you can then ruff your other club loser with the ♠9.

Suppose instead that East ruffs the second round of clubs with a low trump. You will then win his return and draw two rounds of trumps before attempting to ruff your remaining club loser. You will survive when East started with three or fewer trumps and you can therefore draw his remaining trumps in two rounds. Another small chance is that West may hold a singleton ♠J. In that case, East will not be able to overruff dummy's ♠10 when you ruff your club loser.

# CHAPTER 5

# SURVIVING A 4-1 TRUMP BREAK

*I will survive*
Gloria Gaynor

When you have five trumps out against you, they will break 4-1 almost three times in every ten. Quite often this will cause you a problem. In this chapter, we will see some of the ways in which you can protect yourself from such pieces of bad luck.

## DISCARD A LOSER AS THE DEFENDER RUFFS

When the deal below arose in a club duplicate, a surprising number of declarers went down. See what you make of it.

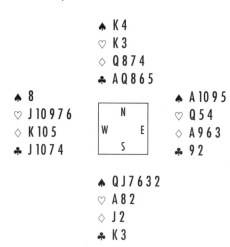

| WEST | NORTH | EAST | SOUTH |
|------|-------|------|-------|
|      | 1♣    | pass | 1♠    |
| pass | 2♣    | pass | 3♠    |
| pass | 4♠    | all pass |   |

How will you play the spade game when West leads the ♡J?

Seeing that the contract was more or less cold on a 3-2 trump break, some declarers won the heart lead and turned immediately to the trump suit. When East took his ♠A, he was quick to switch to a diamond and the defenders scored two tricks in the suit. The 4-1 trump break meant that a second trump trick had to be lost and that was down one.

There is a fair chance of surviving a 4-1 trump break by playing on clubs before trumps. You win the heart lead with the king, cross to the ♡A and ruff a heart with the ♠4. You continue with the king, ace and queen of clubs. If clubs break 3-3, you dispose of a diamond loser and can afford the subsequent loss of two trump tricks. (You do best to continue with a fourth round of clubs, in fact, throwing your last diamond). Even when clubs break 4-2, the play may still gain. When East holds four trumps and a doubleton club, as in the diagram, he will have to ruff with a natural trump trick. You dispose of your diamond loser and subsequently lose one diamond and two trumps.

What if West holds four trumps and a doubleton club? The chances are not so good. West will ruff the third club and may then be able to cross to his partner's hand with a diamond, underleading the ♢A if necessary. A fourth round of clubs is then likely to promote a third trump trick for the defense.

## PREVENT THE DEFENDER FROM DRAWING TRUMPS

You must be particularly careful when your trump holding is A-K-x-x opposite x-x-x-x, or A-x-x-x opposite K-x-x-x. If you draw two rounds of trumps, discovering a 4-1 break, the key defender may gain the lead and be able to draw your remaining trumps. This type of deal is very common:

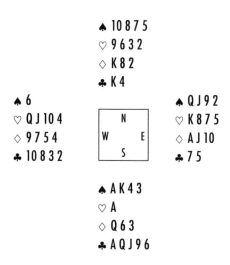

West leads the ♡Q against 4♠ and you win with the ♡A. How will you play?

Suppose your first move is to cash the ace and king of trumps, West showing out on the first round. Can you recover by running your club winners? Not if East is a competent performer. He will refuse to ruff any of your club winners, happily discarding red-suit losers. When you subsequently play a diamond, he will pounce with the ace and draw your remaining trumps with the queen and the jack. Even if you take a heart ruff when in dummy with the ♣K, you will still be one trick short.

How can you avoid this fate? You should draw just one round of trumps and then play a diamond to the king. East wins with the ◇A and forces you with a heart. You ruff, cross to the ♣K and ruff another heart. When you draw a second round of trumps and continue with the ace and queen of clubs, throwing dummy's last heart, East is powerless. If he returns the ◇J, you will win with the ◇Q and throw dummy's last diamond on another good club.

## DUCK A TRUMP WHILE DUMMY'S TRUMPS PROTECT YOU

Suppose you are playing in a 5-3 trump fit with the top three trumps — something like 8-4-2 in the dummy opposite A-K-Q-5-3 in your hand. You may have to lose a trump trick when the suit breaks 4-1. If you can afford to lose a trump trick, it may suit you to duck an early round. By doing so, you will lose the lead when dummy's trumps are still there to protect you.

```
              ♠ 8 4 2
              ♡ 8 5 3
              ◇ 8 6
              ♣ K Q J 9 2
♠ J 10 7 6                      ♠ 9
♡ K Q J 2        ┌─────────┐    ♡ 10 9 7 6 4
◇ K 5 4         │ N       │    ◇ A Q J 7 3
♣ 6 4          W│         │E   ♣ 10 5
                │       S │
                └─────────┘
              ♠ A K Q 5 3
              ♡ A
              ◇ 10 9 2
              ♣ A 8 7 3
```

| WEST | NORTH | EAST | SOUTH |
|------|-------|------|-------|
|      |       |      | 1♠    |
| pass | 2♠    | pass | 4♠    |
| all pass |    |      |       |

West leads the ♡K against your spade game. How will you play the contract?

Suppose you win with the singleton ace and cash the ace and king of trumps, East showing out. You will go down! Turning to the club suit will not save you, because West will delay his ruff until the fourth round; he will then exit with his last trump and you will be left with three diamond losers.

You can afford to lose two diamonds and one trump. After winning the heart lead, you should draw one round of trumps with the ace and then lead a low trump. West wins with the ♠10, but he cannot damage you. There is still one trump in the dummy, preventing the defenders from scoring three diamond tricks. You will win West's return, draw the outstanding trumps and play five rounds of clubs, discarding one of your diamond losers.

## DEVELOP A SIDE SUIT WHILE DUMMY'S TRUMPS PROTECT YOU

When the defenders embark on a 'forcing defense', their aim is to force you to ruff in the long-trump hand. If the adverse trumps break 4-1 and the defenders can reduce your trump length to less than theirs, you will lose control of the deal. What can you do to avoid such an outcome? You must try to absorb the force in the short-trump hand, usually the dummy. Look at this deal:

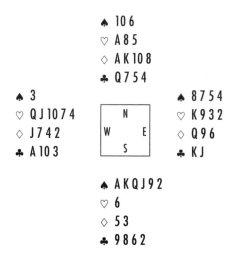

♠ 10 6
♡ A 8 5
◇ A K 10 8
♣ Q 7 5 4

♠ 3
♡ Q J 10 7 4
◇ J 7 4 2
♣ A 10 3

♠ 8 7 5 4
♡ K 9 3 2
◇ Q 9 6
♣ K J

♠ A K Q J 9 2
♡ 6
◇ 5 3
♣ 9 8 6 2

| WEST | NORTH | EAST | SOUTH |
|------|-------|------|-------|
|  | 1♣ | pass | 1♠ |
| pass | 1NT | pass | 4♠ |
| all pass | | | |

West leads the ♡Q against your spade game. How will you play the contract?

Suppose you 'do what comes naturally', winning with the ♡A and drawing two rounds of trumps. When trumps prove to be 4-1, you will go down! You need to establish a club trick to bring your total to ten. Each time you concede a trick in clubs, the defenders will force you with a heart. Whether or not you draw East's remaining trumps before playing on clubs, you will lose control of the deal and go down.

The best idea on this type of hand is to attack the side suit immediately, leaving dummy's trumps intact to help you to rebuff the forcing defense. So, after winning the first trick with the ♡A, you lead a club from dummy. East wins and forces you with a heart. You play another club, East winning, and again ruff the heart return. What can West do when he wins the third round of clubs? All he can do is shake his head! If he plays yet another heart, you will be able to ruff with dummy's ♠10 and draw the outstanding trumps.

# FORCE THE DEFENDER TO RUFF WITH THE FOURTH TRUMP

When dummy holds three trumps to one or more honors, many a contract can be made by establishing a side suit in dummy and then 'drawing trumps, ending in the dummy'. You cannot do this, of course, when a defender holds four trumps. In that case, though, it may be possible to shorten the defender's trumps and then draw his last trump as you cross to the dummy. Let's see an example:

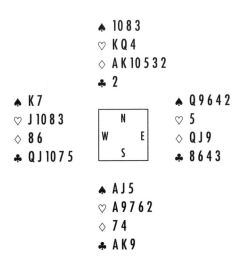

```
              ♠ 10 8 3
              ♡ K Q 4
              ◇ A K 10 5 3 2
              ♣ 2
♠ K 7                          ♠ Q 9 6 4 2
♡ J 10 8 3         N          ♡ 5
◇ 8 6         W         E     ◇ Q J 9
♣ Q J 10 7 5        S          ♣ 8 6 4 3
              ♠ A J 5
              ♡ A 9 7 6 2
              ◇ 7 4
              ♣ A K 9
```

West leads the ♣Q against your small slam in hearts. How will you play?

You need to set up the diamonds and they will almost certainly have to break 3-2. What about the trumps? A 3-2 break would be nice, as always. (You could then draw trumps in three rounds and duck a round of diamonds.) You would like to succeed when a defender holds four trumps. Can it be done?

You should cash the ace of trumps and then play two top diamonds. Both defenders follow, you are pleased to see, and you continue with another diamond, ruffing with the ♡9 in your hand. What can West do? If he overruffs, you can win his return and 'draw trumps, ending in the dummy'. It will then be a simple matter to run the established diamonds, discarding three black-suit losers. Nor will West fare any better by refusing to overruff. You will then cross to the king of trumps and play winning diamonds until West ruffs. Again, you will be able to win his return, draw the last trump with dummy's king and score any remaining diamonds. It was essential to retain two trump entries to the dummy (to deal with the case where trumps are 4-1 and the defender refuses to overruff the third diamond).

## Using a Trump Coup to Pick Up the Four-Card Holding

When your trump holding is something like A-Q-5-4 opposite K-10-7-2, you must begin by cashing the ace and queen. If the defender in the second seat holds J-x-x-x, you can pick up his holding with a simple finesse of the ten. It is not so easy when your trumps are K-3 opposite A-Q-10-8-6-5. By the time you have discovered J-x-x-x onside, it is too late to take a finesse. It may still be possible to avoid a trump loser by arranging to be in dummy at Trick 12, with the Q-10 of trumps sitting over the defender's J-9. When you lead a plain card towards your hand, or arrange for the left-hand defender to do this, you will avoid losing a trump trick.

Let's see a trump coup where you have to take special care with the entries.

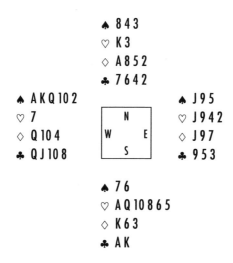

| WEST | NORTH | EAST | SOUTH |
|------|-------|------|-------|
| 1♠ | pass | pass | 3♡ |
| pass | 4♡ | all pass | |

West leads the ♠K and switches to the ♣Q. How will you play ?

You have three certain losers in spades and diamonds, so all depends on picking up the trump suit without loss. Before playing another trick, you must pause to think how you could deal with East holding ♡J-x-x-x. You will need to take two black-suit ruffs in your hand to shorten your trumps to the same length as East's. You will then exit with a third round of diamonds, forcing the defenders to give you the last two tricks with the ♡Q-10. How can this be done?

At Trick 3, you surrender a second spade trick, preparing for a spade ruff in your hand. West wins and plays another club to your king. Now you play the ace and king of trumps, cashing the honors in this order, so that you will be in dummy (to take a spade ruff) in the dangerous case where East holds ♡J-x-x-x. West does indeed show out and you ruff a spade in your hand. You continue with the king and ace of diamonds and lead a club from dummy, ruffing with the ♡8.

Your last three cards are the ♡Q-10 and a losing diamond. You exit with the diamond and are guaranteed to score the last two tricks with your trump tenace.

An inexperienced West might have assisted you in reducing your trumps by playing three top spades at the beginning. When West refused to do this, switching to clubs, you had to do the hard work yourself.

If you like to extract the maximum mileage from each deal, you can give East all five trumps, in a hand such as

♠ J 9 5   ♡ J 9 7 4 2   ◇ J 9 7   ♣ 9 5

The recommended line of play still lands the contract. As before, you will score four side-suit winners and six trump tricks.

**1**

♠ 8 3 2
♡ 9 7 4 2
◇ A K Q J 10 3
♣ —

♣ K led

♠ A Q 4
♡ A K Q 6
◇ 7 4
♣ 9 6 5 3

| WEST | NORTH | EAST | SOUTH |
|------|-------|------|-------|
|      | 1◇    | pass | 1♡    |
| pass | 4♣    | pass | 6♡    |
| all pass |    |      |       |

You bid to 6♡ and West leads the ♣K. How will you play the contract?

**2**

♠ 9 7 6 4
♡ A K 7
◇ 10 5
♣ A Q 7 4

◇ 4 led

♠ A K 5 2
♡ J 8 4
◇ 7
♣ K J 9 6 2

| WEST | NORTH | EAST | SOUTH |
|------|-------|------|-------|
|      | 1♣    | 1♡   | 1♠    |
| pass | 2♠    | 3◇   | 4♠    |
| all pass |    |      |       |

West leads the ◇4 against your spade game. How will you play the hand?

**3**

♠ A 10 7 4
♡ A K
♢ 6 4 2
♣ A K 8 6

◇ 3 led

♠ 2
♡ Q J 8 6 3 2
♢ Q 7
♣ 9 7 5 4

| WEST | NORTH | EAST | SOUTH |
|------|-------|------|-------|
|  | 1♣ | 1◇ | 1♡ |
| pass | 2NT | pass | 4♡ |
| all pass |  |  |  |

West leads the ◇3. East wins with the ◇K and continues with the ◇A, West following with the ◇8. East persists with another diamond. How will you play?

**4**

♠ 9 8 4
♡ A 5 2
♢ A Q J 4
♣ Q 6 5

♣ J led

♠ A K 6 3
♡ K Q 8 6 3
♢ K 7
♣ 8 4

| WEST | NORTH | EAST | SOUTH |
|------|-------|------|-------|
|  |  |  | 1♡ |
| pass | 2◇ | pass | 2♠ |
| pass | 4♡ | all pass |  |

West leads the ♣J. He continues with another club, East winning with the ♣K and then playing the ♣A. You ruff low and West follows suit. How will you continue?

1

```
              ♠ 8 3 2
              ♡ 9 7 4 2
              ◇ A K Q J 10 3
              ♣ —
♠ K 7 5                        ♠ J 10 9 6
♡ J 10 8 3        N           ♡ 5
◇ 6          W         E       ◇ 9 8 5 2
♣ K Q J 10 7       S          ♣ A 8 4 2
              ♠ A Q 4
              ♡ A K Q 6
              ◇ 7 4
              ♣ 9 6 5 3
```

| WEST | NORTH | EAST | SOUTH |
|------|-------|------|-------|
|  | 1◇ | pass | 1♡ |
| pass | 4♣ | pass | 6♡ |
| all pass |  |  |  |

West leads the ♣K against your small slam in hearts. How will you play?

The first question to ask yourself is: can you survive a 4-1 trump break? If you have to lose a trump trick, you will score three trump tricks in the South hand, six diamond tricks and the ♠A. That is a total of ten, so you will still make the slam if you can ruff two clubs in the dummy.

Suppose you ruff the club lead, cross to the ♡A and ruff another club. When you play dummy's last trump to your king, East will show out. The slam can no longer be made. West will use his trump winner to ruff the second round of diamonds, preventing you from scoring more than one trick in the suit.

You can afford to lose a trump trick, but you must do so at a time when you still have a trump in dummy to protect you from the defenders' clubs. You should therefore duck a trump at Trick 2. West has no constructive return to make. If he plays back a trump, you will win, take another club ruff and return to your hand with the ♠A to draw trumps. You will then make the twelve tricks that we visualized above.

As it happens, a diamond lead would have beaten the slam. You would not have sufficient entries to the South hand to score two club ruffs, duck a trump and draw the outstanding trumps. The lead of a trump honor would also have defeated you.

```
                    ♠ 9 7 6 4
                    ♡ A K 7
                    ◇ 10 5
                    ♣ A Q 7 4
    ♠ Q J 10 3                      ♠ 8
    ♡ 5 3            ┌─────────┐    ♡ Q 10 9 6 2
    ◇ J 9 6 4 3     │   N     │    ◇ A K Q 8 2
    ♣ 10 8          │ W     E │    ♣ 5 3
                    │   S     │
                    └─────────┘
                    ♠ A K 5 2
                    ♡ J 8 4
                    ◇ 7
                    ♣ K J 9 6 2
```

| WEST | NORTH | EAST | SOUTH |
|------|-------|------|-------|
|      | 1♣    | 1♡   | 1♠    |
| pass | 2♠    | 3◇   | 4♠    |
| all pass |   |      |       |

West, with his chunky trump holding, is not interested in ruffs and prefers a diamond lead to a heart. East wins and continues with a second top diamond, which you ruff. What now?

Let's suppose first that you draw two rounds of trumps with the ace and king. East will show out on the second round — no great surprise after his bidding in the red suits — and you will be in trouble. The best you can do is run the club suit, but West will delay his ruff until the fourth round of the suit. He will then play his remaining trump. There will be no way to avoid a heart loser and that will be down one.

The correct way to play the hand is to draw just one round of trumps, with the ace, and then to turn to the club suit. It will do West no good to delay his ruff until the fourth round. You can win his trump return with the king and play a fifth round of clubs, discarding dummy's heart loser. It makes no difference whether West chooses to ruff this with his master trump. You will lose just two trumps and one diamond.

What if trumps had been 3-2 all along? Following this line would then cost you an overtrick. That's the same with many safety plays.

**3**

```
                        ♠ A 10 7 4
                        ♡ A K
                        ◊ 6 4 2
                        ♣ A K 8 6
  ♠ Q 8 5 3                              ♠ K J 9 6
  ♡ 10 9 5 4          ┌─────────┐        ♡ 7
  ◊ J 8 3             │    N    │        ◊ A K 10 9 5
  ♣ J 3               │ W     E │        ♣ Q 10 2
                      │    S    │
                      └─────────┘
                        ♠ 2
                        ♡ Q J 8 6 3 2
                        ◊ Q 7
                        ♣ 9 7 5 4
```

| WEST | NORTH | EAST | SOUTH |
|------|-------|------|-------|
|      | 1♣    | 1◊   | 1♡    |
| pass | 2NT   | pass | 4♡    |
| all pass |   |      |       |

West leads the ◊3 against your game in hearts. East wins with the ◊K and continues with the ◊A, West following with the ◊8. East then plays another diamond. How will you play?

You ruff with a low trump and West follows with the ◊J. Suppose your next move is to cash dummy's two trump honors. East will show out on the second round and you will be in trouble. You cannot afford to reach your hand with a spade ruff to draw trumps, because this would exhaust your own trump holding. You would therefore have to play ace, king and another club before drawing trumps. East would win the third round of clubs and a further round of diamonds would promote a trump trick for West.

How can you preserve trump control? Play a trump to the ace if you like, but you must set up the clubs while the ♡K is still in dummy. A fourth round of diamonds from East would then do you no damage. You would ruff low in the South hand. If West chose to overruff, you would overruff again with dummy's ♡K. Whether or not West chose to overruff the fourth round of diamonds, you would be able to draw trumps and make the remaining tricks.

If East returns a spade instead, after taking his club trick, you can win and draw trumps, making the contract easily.

```
                    ♠ 9 8 4
                    ♡ A 5 2
                    ◇ A Q J 4
                    ♣ Q 6 5
    ♠ Q 5                           ♠ J 10 7 2
    ♡ J 10 7 4          N           ♡ 9
    ◇ 9 3          W         E      ◇ 10 8 6 5 2
    ♣ J 10 9 3 2        S           ♣ A K 7
                    ♠ A K 6 3
                    ♡ K Q 8 6 3
                    ◇ K 7
                    ♣ 8 4
```

| WEST | NORTH | EAST | SOUTH |
|------|-------|------|-------|
|      |       |      | 1♡    |
| pass | 2◇    | pass | 2♠    |
| pass | 4♡    | all pass |   |

West leads the ♣J against your game in hearts. He continues with another club, East winning with the ♣K and then playing the ♣A. You ruff low and West follows suit. How will you continue?

You should cash the king and queen of trumps. If the suit breaks 3-2, you draw the last trump and score an easy overtrick. When East shows out on the second round of trumps, you turn to the diamond suit, planning to throw spade losers from your hand. Suppose West ruffs the third round of diamonds and returns another club. You can ruff in the South hand and draw the last trump with dummy's ace. If instead West declines to ruff, you can draw one more round of trumps and then play your remaining diamond and spade winners. Either way you will score ten tricks and make your game.

## CHAPTER 6

# EXTRACTING THE SAFE EXIT CARDS

*No place to go*
Warren Brothers

In this chapter, we will look at various contracts that can be made with an eventual throw-in play. In particular, we will see how you can set up successful end positions by extracting the defenders' safe exit cards.

## RUFFING OUT THE EXIT CARDS

On the first deal, your victim's safe exit cards in clubs are removed by taking some ruffs in the suit.

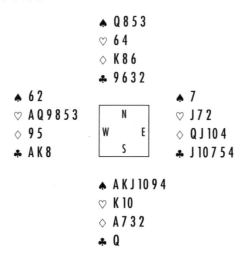

```
              ♠ Q853
              ♡ 64
              ◇ K86
              ♣ 9632
♠ 62                        ♠ 7
♡ AQ9853        N           ♡ J72
◇ 95          W   E         ◇ QJ104
♣ AK8           S           ♣ J10754
              ♠ AKJ1094
              ♡ K10
              ◇ A732
              ♣ Q
```

| WEST | NORTH | EAST | SOUTH |
|------|-------|------|-------|
|      |       |      | 1♠    |
| 2♡   | 2♠    | pass | 4♠    |
| all pass |   |      |       |

A trump lead would have proved effective, as it happens, but West makes the natural lead of the ♣A. When East plays the ♣4 and the ♣Q falls from declarer, he switches to the ♠2. How would you tackle the contract?

A 3-3 diamond break will not necessarily give you the contract, because if East gains the lead on the third round of the suit, he can lead through your ♡K. Your best hope is that West holds only two diamonds in a hand of 2-6-2-3 (or 1-7-2-3) shape. You win the trump switch with dummy's ♠8 and ruff a club in your hand, removing one of West's safe exit cards. You cross to the ♠Q, West following with the outstanding trump, and ruff another club.

West's safe exit cards in clubs have been removed. You continue with the ace and king of diamonds, West producing the ◇5 and the ◇9. These cards remain:

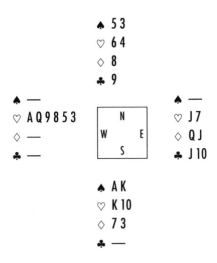

```
              ♠ 5 3
              ♡ 6 4
              ◇ 8
              ♣ 9
♠ —                          ♠ —
♡ A Q 9 8 5 3    N           ♡ J 7
◇ —           W     E        ◇ Q J
♣ —              S           ♣ J 10
              ♠ A K
              ♡ K 10
              ◇ 7 3
              ♣ —
```

If West began with 2-5-3-3 shape and has carelessly retained the ◇Q, you can make your contract now by playing a diamond. This is very unlikely, though. With four-card support, East might have raised hearts and West would surely have unblocked the ◇Q if he held it. So, confident in your card-reading, you play a heart from dummy instead. Whichever card East chooses to play, you cover it. West scores two heart tricks and then has to give you a ruff-and-sluff. Away goes dummy's diamond loser and you ruff your two diamond losers in the dummy.

## DUCK A ROUND TO REMOVE THE EXIT CARD

On the next deal, you must employ a different technique. You must duck an early round of the suit in which you hope to remove a defender's safe exit card.

```
              ♠ 6 5 2
              ♡ K 6 5
              ◇ A K 4 3
              ♣ 8 6 4
  ♠ Q J 10 9 3              ♠ 8 4
  ♡ 8 2          ┌─────┐     ♡ Q J 10 9 3
  ◇ J 9 8 6      │ N   │     ◇ 2
  ♣ J 3        W │     │ E   ♣ K Q 10 9 5
                 │   S │
                 └─────┘
              ♠ A K 7
              ♡ A 7 4
              ◇ Q 10 7 5
              ♣ A 7 2
```

| WEST | NORTH | EAST | SOUTH |
|------|-------|------|-------|
|      |       |      | 1NT   |
| pass | 3NT   | all pass |   |

West leads the ♠Q and you win with the ♠A. When you continue with the ace and king of diamonds, a small problem arises. West holds ◇J-9-x-x and you have only three tricks in the suit. How will you continue?

You must aim to throw West in with the third round of spades at a time when he can cash a total of only four winners and will then have to lead into your diamond tenace. Since you are missing seven cards in both hearts and clubs, West's most likely shape in those suits is 2-2. To make sure that West does not have a safe exit card in clubs, you should now duck a round of clubs.

You win the return, whatever it may be, and cash your remaining winners in hearts and clubs. Since West did indeed start with two hearts and two clubs, you have now stripped his safe exit cards. When you throw him in with the third round of spades, he cashes two spade winners and then surveys the last two cards in his hand, the ◇J-9. With a sympathetic look in your eye, you show him your ◇Q-10 and claim the last two tricks.

If West held three hearts and one club, you could make the contract by ducking a heart instead. Playing this way, you would go down when West's shape is 5-2-4-2, however. The defenders would clear the spade suit and you could no longer duck a club. If you cashed the ace and king of hearts, West would throw a spade to keep his safe exit card in clubs. So, you really do need to guess what shape the West hand is. There are 441 possible holdings for West that contain two hearts and two clubs and only 245 where he has three hearts and one club. The odds are therefore 9-to-5 in favor of playing him for 5-2-4-2 shape.

## Forcing a defender to discard an exit card

Next, let's see how you can force a defender to surrender his safe exit cards. Here is the first example of this style of play:

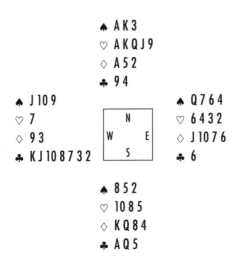

|  ♠ A K 3 |
|  ♡ A K Q J 9 |
|  ◇ A 5 2 |
|  ♣ 9 4 |

| WEST | NORTH | EAST | SOUTH |
|---|---|---|---|
| 3♣ | dbl | pass | 3NT |
| pass | 4NT | pass | 6NT |
| all pass | | | |

The exact nature of limit-bid auctions in notrump after an enemy preempt tends to be undiscussed. Still, the North-South bidding here is not far off the mark and 6NT is a worthwhile contract. How will you tackle it when West leads the jack of spades?

There are eleven top tricks and an even diamond break will give you a stress-free twelfth trick. What if the diamonds fail to divide evenly? It may be possible to strip West of his non-clubs and then endplay him with the ♣9.

You win the spade lead in dummy and cash just four rounds of hearts, finding that West began with a singleton. You throw a spade from your hand and West discards three clubs. You then test the diamonds, playing king, queen and ace. It is no surprise when West shows out on the third round, throwing yet another club. You have a count on West's red suits and it is reasonable to place him with an initial seven clubs for his preempt. In that case the end position will not be a million miles away from this:

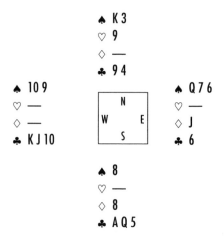

```
              ♠ K 3
              ♡ 9
              ◇ —
              ♣ 9 4
  ♠ 10 9                      ♠ Q 7 6
  ♡ —          N             ♡ —
  ◇ —       W     E          ◇ J
  ♣ K J 10      S            ♣ 6
              ♠ 8
              ♡ —
              ◇ 8
              ♣ A Q 5
```

You cash dummy's last heart, discarding the ◇8 from your hand. What can West do? If he throws a club, you will run the ♣9 to his hand, setting up an extra trick for yourself in the club suit. West is therefore forced to part with a spade, which was his intended safe exit card. You cash the ♠K, stripping West of his non-clubs. You lead the ♣9 and your last worry vanishes when East's singleton club is a lowly six-spot. You contribute the ♣5 from your hand and West has to win and lead back into your ♣A-Q. Slam made!

Here is another deal where a defender is put to an awkward discard before being thrown in. In one suit, he is forced to reduce to a singleton honor. A losing finesse is then taken to it, leaving him endplayed.

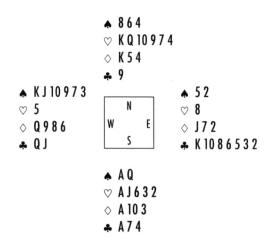

```
              ♠ 8 6 4
              ♡ K Q 10 9 7 4
              ◇ K 5 4
              ♣ 9
  ♠ K J 10 9 7 3              ♠ 5 2
  ♡ 5          N             ♡ 8
  ◇ Q 9 8 6  W     E         ◇ J 7 2
  ♣ Q J        S            ♣ K 10 8 6 5 3 2
              ♠ A Q
              ♡ A J 6 3 2
              ◇ A 10 3
              ♣ A 7 4
```

| WEST | NORTH | EAST | SOUTH |
|------|-------|------|-------|
|      |       |      | 1♡    |
| 2♠   | 4♣    | pass | 6♡    |
| all pass |   |      |       |

West leads the ♣Q against your small slam in hearts. You win with the ace, ruff a club high, cross to the ♡J and ruff your last club. An obvious start, yes, but how will you continue?

If West began with ◇Q-J-x(-x), he can be endplayed on the third round of diamonds. He will not prosper by unblocking the queen and the jack on the first two rounds, because your ◇10 will then become good. However, it is a small chance to find him with both missing diamond honors and you would like to make the contract when he has only one diamond honor. Do you see how this can be done?

You must run the trump suit to put pressure on West. This will be the position with one trump still to be played:

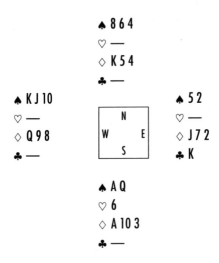

```
              ♠ 8 6 4
              ♡ —
              ◇ K 5 4
              ♣ —
 ♠ K J 10                    ♠ 5 2
 ♡ —          ┌─────────┐    ♡ —
 ◇ Q 9 8      │    N    │    ◇ J 7 2
 ♣ —          │ W     E │    ♣ K
              │    S    │
              └─────────┘
              ♠ A Q
              ♡ 6
              ◇ A 10 3
              ♣ —
```

West has shown out of hearts and clubs. At this stage, on the assumption that he began with six spades for his weak jump overcall, you can place him with three spades and three diamonds. If you simply play two top diamonds and exit with a third round of the suit, West can avoid the endplay by unblocking the ◇Q at some stage. Instead, you must cash your last trump. West cannot afford to throw a spade or you will play the ace and queen of spades, setting up a third-round spade winner in the dummy. He therefore has to release a diamond. Let's say that he throws the ◇8. You lead a diamond to West's ◇9 and dummy's ◇ K. Then you play a low diamond from dummy, finessing the ◇ 10. West wins with the singleton ◇ Q and has to lead into your spade tenace, giving you the slam.

It was an unusual position in diamonds. West was not squeezed out of the sole stopper in the suit, but he was forced to bare an honor that was not a master. You were then able to finesse into that card, leaving him endplayed.

## COUNTING THE HAND TO DIAGNOSE A THROW-IN PLAY

Obtaining a complete count on the hand is often essential when planning a throw-in. It is not difficult on the next deal, because one of the opponents has made a preemptive opening bid.

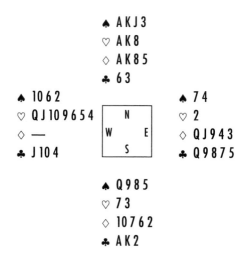

| WEST | NORTH | EAST | SOUTH |
|------|-------|------|-------|
| 3♡ | dbl | pass | 4♠ |
| pass | 6♠ | all pass | |

You win the ♡Q lead in dummy and draw trumps in three rounds, surprised to see that West holds three trumps. You cash the ◇A, hoping to see a singleton honor appear from West. No, he shows out, throwing a heart. How will you continue?

You have a complete count on the East hand. He began with 2-1-5-5 shape, so both defenders hold a club guard and a simple squeeze will not be possible. What else can you try? If you can strip East of his clubs, you can lead a diamond towards the ten in a three-card ending. How can this be done?

You can cash the top clubs, if you like, and then play a heart to the king. This will be the position:

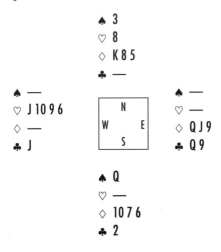

```
            ♠ 3
            ♡ 8
            ◊ K 8 5
            ♣ —
♠ —                        ♠ —
♡ J 10 9 6      N          ♡ —
◊ —         W       E      ◊ Q J 9
♣ J             S          ♣ Q 9
            ♠ Q
            ♡ —
            ◊ 10 7 6
            ♣ 2
```

East has already been forced to release one of his precious clubs. You ruff a heart in your hand and this pries another club from the East hand. (If he threw a diamond instead, of course, you would duck a round of that suit, setting up a long diamond.) East now has only one club and you can remove that by ruffing the ♣2 in dummy. You are down to the three-card ending that you visualized when the diamond situation first came to light. When you lead a low diamond from dummy, East has to rise with one honor and lead away from the other. The slam is yours.

Here is another throw-in deal where counting will assist you:

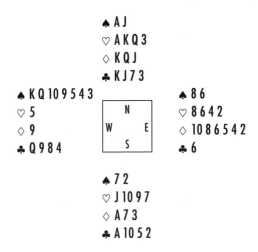

```
                  ♠ A J
                  ♡ A K Q 3
                  ◊ K Q J
                  ♣ K J 7 3
♠ K Q 10 9 5 4 3                    ♠ 8 6
♡ 5              N                  ♡ 8 6 4 2
◊ 9          W       E             ◊ 10 8 6 5 4 2
♣ Q 9 8 4        S                 ♣ 6
                  ♠ 7 2
                  ♡ J 10 9 7
                  ◊ A 7 3
                  ♣ A 10 5 2
```

| WEST | NORTH | EAST | SOUTH |
|------|-------|------|-------|
| 3♠ | dbl | pass | 4♡ |
| pass | 5♡ | pass | 6♡ |
| all pass | | | |

Holding 24 points, North judges that his hand is worth a slam try. With two aces, you are happy to accept, and the ♠K is led. You win with dummy's ace and play two rounds of trumps, finding West with a singleton. How will you continue?

You draw East's remaining trumps and now need to score four club tricks to make the slam. With West holding eight cards in the majors to East's six, the odds favor East to hold the majority of the clubs and therefore the ♣Q. There is no need to take an immediate view of the clubs, however, because three rounds of diamonds will provide further information. When you cash the king and queen of diamonds, West throws a spade on the second round. Ah, that changes the situation!

West is now marked with 7-1-1-4 shape. You cash the ♣A in order to extract East's singleton in the suit and then finesse the ♣J, East showing out. So far so good. These cards are left:

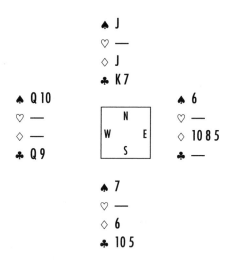

```
                    ♠ J
                    ♡ —
                    ♢ J
                    ♣ K 7
  ♠ Q 10                         ♠ 6
  ♡ —          ┌─────────┐       ♡ —
  ♢ —          │    N    │       ♢ 10 8 5
  ♣ Q 9        │ W     E │       ♣ —
               │    S    │
               └─────────┘
                    ♠ 7
                    ♡ —
                    ♢ 6
                    ♣ 10 5
```

You lead the ♢J from dummy and West is trapped in the headlights. No subterfuge is possible, because you have a certain count on the deal. When West discards the ♠10, you throw him in with the ♠Q so he has to lead into your split club tenace. Small slam bid; small slam made.

## Extracting the link to partner's winner

We will end the chapter by looking at a type of deal where you need to concede a round of a suit in order to set up an extra winner. You cannot do it immediately, because the defender who won the trick would then be able to cross to a winner or two in his partner's hand. First, you must extract the defender's cards in his partner's suit. Take a look at this deal:

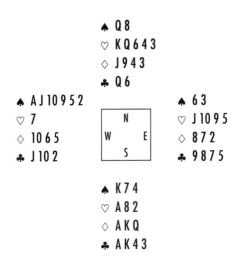

```
                    ♠ Q 8
                    ♡ K Q 6 4 3
                    ◇ J 9 4 3
                    ♣ Q 6
  ♠ A J 10 9 5 2              ♠ 6 3
  ♡ 7              N          ♡ J 10 9 5
  ◇ 10 6 5      W     E       ◇ 8 7 2
  ♣ J 10 2         S          ♣ 9 8 7 5
                    ♠ K 7 4
                    ♡ A 8 2
                    ◇ A K Q
                    ♣ A K 4 3
```

| WEST | NORTH | EAST | SOUTH |
|------|-------|------|-------|
| 2♠ | pass | pass | dbl |
| pass | 4♡ | pass | 4NT |
| pass | 5♣ | pass | 6NT |
| all pass | | | |

North's 5♣ response to Roman Keycard Blackwood shows one keycard, the king of the temporarily agreed trump suit. West leads the ♣J against the resultant small slam in notrump. How will you play the contract?

You must win with the ♣Q, avoiding any unseemly blockage in the club suit. You then cash the top three diamonds in your hand and lead a low spade towards the dummy. West cannot afford to rise with the ♠A or you will have two spade tricks — enough for the contract — so dummy's ♠Q wins the trick. When you continue with the ◇J, poor East comes under pressure in three suits. Since he cannot afford to release a heart or a club, he can delay his fate only by discarding his last spade.

You play a heart to the ace and lead a second heart towards dummy. If West follows suit, you will score five heart tricks and end with an overtrick. When West in fact shows out, you duck in the dummy, allowing East to win the trick. You have established an extra heart trick in dummy and still have an entry in the suit. East, meanwhile has no spade to play. He lamely returns a heart or a club and you claim the remaining tricks.

**1**

♠ 8 5
♡ 8 4 2
♦ Q 7
♣ 9 8 7 5 4 3

♣Q led

♠ A K Q J 10 7
♡ A J 10
♦ A K 3
♣ A

| WEST | NORTH | EAST | SOUTH |
|------|-------|------|-------|
| 2♡ | pass | pass | dbl |
| pass | 2NT | pass | 6♠ |
| all pass | | | |

How will you play the spade slam when West leads the ♣Q?

**2**

♠ K Q 5
♡ A K 10 7 6
♦ Q 7 5
♣ K 6

♣Q led

♠ A 7 6 4
♡ Q J 9 5
♦ A 9 3
♣ A 8

| WEST | NORTH | EAST | SOUTH |
|------|-------|------|-------|
| | | 3♦ | dbl |
| pass | 4♦ | pass | 4♡ |
| pass | 5♡ | pass | 6♡ |
| all pass | | | |

West leads the ♣Q. It looks like a simple elimination deal, but when you play a round of trumps, East shows out. How can you recover the situation?

**3**

```
            ♠ 8 4 2
            ♡ 9 8 7 2
            ◇ 9 4 2
            ♣ 9 5 4

  ♣2 led

            ♠ A K Q J 10 5
            ♡ A K J 5
            ◇ A 8 5
            ♣ —
```

| WEST | NORTH | EAST | SOUTH |
|------|-------|------|-------|
|      |       | 1♣   | dbl   |
| 1♡   | pass  | 2♣   | 4♠    |
| all pass | | | |

West leads the ♣2 against your spade game. How will you play? (Trumps break 2-2.)

**4**

```
            ♠ 6 5
            ♡ Q 8 6 5
            ◇ A K 4
            ♣ A Q 8 6

  ♠K led

            ♠ A 10 7
            ♡ A 7 4
            ◇ 8 7 5
            ♣ K J 7 2
```

| WEST | NORTH | EAST | SOUTH |
|------|-------|------|-------|
| 1♠   | dbl   | pass | 2NT   |
| pass | 3NT   | all pass | |

West leads the ♠K against 3NT. How will you play the contract?

# ANSWERS

1

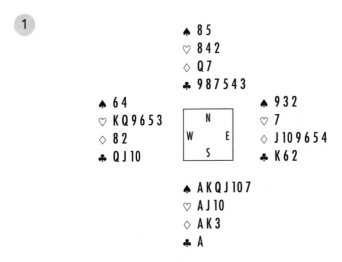

```
              ♠ 8 5
              ♡ 8 4 2
              ◇ Q 7
              ♣ 9 8 7 5 4 3
♠ 6 4                        ♠ 9 3 2
♡ K Q 9 6 5 3      N         ♡ 7
◇ 8 2           W     E      ◇ J 10 9 6 5 4
♣ Q J 10           S         ♣ K 6 2
              ♠ A K Q J 10 7
              ♡ A J 10
              ◇ A K 3
              ♣ A
```

| WEST | NORTH | EAST | SOUTH |
|------|-------|------|-------|
| 2♡ | pass | pass | dbl |
| pass | 2NT | pass | 6♠ |
| all pass | | | |

North's Lebensohl 2NT shows a weak hand in response to the takeout double. Judging that your splendid collection was not designed for a mere game contract, you leap to 6♠. How will you play this contract when West leads the ♣Q?

One possibility, not a very good one, is to play three rounds of diamonds, discarding a heart from dummy. Your aim would be to continue with ace and another heart, eventually ruffing your third heart with dummy's ♠8. Several things could go wrong with this plan. The main problem is that East is the favorite to hold the ♠9 and will then be able to overruff the dummy. Also, as the cards lie, West would ruff the third round of diamonds.

A better idea is to aim to strip West of his non-heart cards and then to end-play him in the heart suit. Draw one round of trumps with the ace and cross to dummy with the ◇Q. You then ruff a club with the ♠7 and cash the ◇A. To reach dummy for a second time, you must ruff the ◇K with dummy's ♠8. West is out of diamonds, as it happens, but he does not hold the ♠9. You ruff a club with the ♠10, removing West's last safe exit card. The way is now clear for you to draw the outstanding trumps and exit with the ♡J. West has to win with one of his honors and then lead back into your ♡A-10 tenace.

♠ K Q 5
♡ A K 10 7 6
◇ Q 7 5
♣ K 6

♠ J 9 8 3
♡ 8 4 3 2
◇ —
♣ Q J 10 5 2

```
        N
    W       E
        S
```

♠ 10 2
♡ —
◇ K J 10 8 6 4 2
♣ 9 7 4 3

♠ A 7 6 4
♡ Q J 9 5
◇ A 9 3
♣ A 8

| WEST | NORTH | EAST | SOUTH |
|------|-------|------|-------|
|  |  | 3◇ | dbl |
| pass | 4◇ | pass | 4♡ |
| pass | 5♡ | pass | 6♡ |
| all pass |  |  |  |

West leads the ♣Q and you win with the ♣A. It looks like a simple elimination hand (draw trumps, eliminate the black suits and duck a diamond to endplay East). When you play a trump to the ace, however, East shows out. How will you continue?

If spades break 3-3, you will have a discard for one of dummy's diamond losers. Otherwise, you must aim to strip East of his black cards and then endplay him by ducking a diamond.

You draw all the trumps and play three rounds of spades. If East began with four spades, you can strip his clubs and throw him in with a spade, discarding a diamond from dummy (or ruff the spade and duck a diamond). When instead East began with four clubs, his last five cards will be ◇K-J-10 ♣9-8. You must ruff your last spade in dummy and East has to release a club (otherwise, you can duck a diamond and set up an extra diamond trick by length). You can then strip East's last club by cashing dummy's king, and duck a diamond to endplay him.

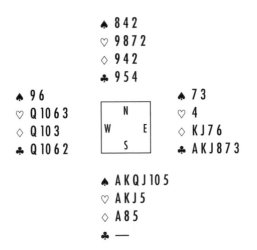

③

|  |  | ♠ 8 4 2 |  |
|  |  | ♡ 9 8 7 2 |  |
|  |  | ◇ 9 4 2 |  |
|  |  | ♣ 9 5 4 |  |

| ♠ 9 6 |  |  | ♠ 7 3 |
| ♡ Q 10 6 3 | N |  | ♡ 4 |
| ◇ Q 10 3 | W   E |  | ◇ K J 7 6 |
| ♣ Q 10 6 2 | S |  | ♣ A K J 8 7 3 |

|  |  | ♠ A K Q J 10 5 |  |
|  |  | ♡ A K J 5 |  |
|  |  | ◇ A 8 5 |  |
|  |  | ♣ — |  |

| WEST | NORTH | EAST | SOUTH |
|------|-------|------|-------|
|      |       | 1♣   | dbl   |
| 1♡   | pass  | 2♣   | 4♠    |
| all pass |   |      |       |

West leads the ♣2 against your spade game. How will you play?

Unlikely as it may seem, you must aim to set up an endplay on West. Ruff with the ♠10 and draw trumps in two rounds. Cash the ♡A and play ace and another diamond. If the defenders take two diamond winners and return a club, you will ruff high again. These cards will be left:

|  |  | ♠ 8 |  |
|  |  | ♡ 9 8 7 |  |
|  |  | ◇ — |  |
|  |  | ♣ 9 |  |

| ♠ — |  |  | ♠ — |
| ♡ Q 10 6 |  |  | ♡ — |
| ◇ — |  |  | ◇ J |
| ♣ Q 10 |  |  | ♣ A J 8 3 |

|  |  | ♠ Q 5 |  |
|  |  | ♡ K J 5 |  |
|  |  | ◇ — |  |
|  |  | ♣ — |  |

When you cross to the ♠8, West has to throw a club. You ruff the ♣9, removing West's last club, and endplay him with a low heart.

**4**

```
                    ♠ 6 5
                    ♡ Q 8 6 5
                    ◇ A K 4
                    ♣ A Q 8 6
  ♠ K Q J 9 3 2                      ♠ 8 4
  ♡ K 9 2          ┌──────────┐      ♡ J 10 3
  ◇ Q 10 3         │    N     │      ◇ J 9 6 2
  ♣ 5              │  W    E  │      ♣ 10 9 4 3
                   │    S     │
                   └──────────┘
                    ♠ A 10 7
                    ♡ A 7 4
                    ◇ 8 7 5
                    ♣ K J 7 2
```

| WEST | NORTH | EAST | SOUTH |
|------|-------|------|-------|
| 1♠ | dbl | pass | 2NT |
| pass | 3NT | all pass | |

West, who opened the bidding with 1♠, leads the ♠K against 3NT. How will you play the contract?

Your best chance is to find West with the ♡K. You plan to extract his minor-suit cards and then to endplay him with a spade to lead away from the ♡K. When he holds three diamonds, you can achieve this endplay only by winning the very first round of spades! You continue with three rounds of clubs and reach this position:

```
                    ♠ 6
                    ♡ Q 8 6 5
                    ◇ A K 4
                    ♣ 6
  ♠ Q J 9 3                         ♠ 4
  ♡ K 9            ┌──────────┐      ♡ J 10 3
  ◇ Q 10 3         │    N     │      ◇ J 9 6 2
  ♣ —              │  W    E  │      ♣ 10
                   │    S     │
                   └──────────┘
                    ♠ 10 7
                    ♡ A 7 4
                    ◇ 8 7 5
                    ♣ K
```

What can West discard on the ♣K? If he discards a diamond (his safe exit card, having unblocked the ◊Q), you will cash the ◊A-K and throw West in with a spade to lead away from the ♡K. If instead he pitches another spade, leaving himself with only three spade winners, you will be able to lead towards the ♡K. Had you held up the ♠A at Trick 1, dummy would have had no throw-in card after you cashed the ◊A-K.

# CHAPTER 7

# UNUSUAL AVOIDANCE PLAY

> *Easy to avoid*
> Soul Asylum

You bought a card play book with a picture of a four-wheel drive vehicle on the front cover. You will not, therefore, be expecting to find in this chapter some straightforward examples of finessing or ducking into the safe hand. Yes, I understand. Test yourself on this deal, then:

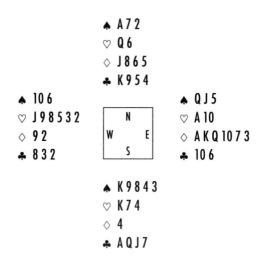

|  | ♠ A 7 2 |  |
|  | ♡ Q 6 |  |
|  | ◇ J 8 6 5 |  |
|  | ♣ K 9 5 4 |  |

| WEST | NORTH | EAST | SOUTH |
|------|-------|------|-------|
|      |       | 1◇   | 1♠    |
| pass | 2◇    | 3◇   | 4♠    |
| all pass |   |      |       |

North's 2◇ shows a sound raise in spades, to at least the two-level. West leads the ◇9 against your spade game and you ruff the second round of the suit. What is your plan?

You would like to ruff a heart in the dummy. Suppose you play a heart to the queen immediately, though. East will win and lead another diamond, promoting a second trump trick for the defenders. To avoid this risk, you should draw two rounds of trumps with the king and the ace. The general idea is then to ruff two more diamonds in the South hand. This will give you five trump tricks (the ace, the king and three ruffs in the South hand) plus four clubs and one heart. East is welcome to ruff one of your club winners, because this will reinstate dummy's remaining trump as your tenth trick.

Suppose you ruff a diamond at Trick 5, cross to the ♣K and ruff another diamond. When you eventually try to establish a heart trick, East will be able to rise with the ace, draw dummy's last trump and cash a diamond trick.

To make the contract, you must therefore lead a heart at Trick 5, through East's ace. If he rises with the ace to draw dummy's last trump, you will have two heart tricks. If instead he plays low, you will pocket the heart trick and continue with the ace and queen of clubs, everyone following. These cards will remain:

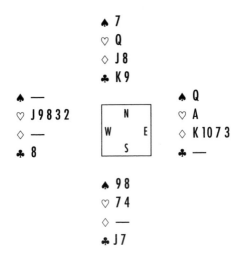

You play the ♣J and overtake with the ♣K. If East ruffs, dummy's ♠7 will be available for a heart ruff. If instead East discards, you have an entry for a diamond ruff. You then overtake the ♣7 with the ♣9, leaving East in the same predicament. If he again declines to ruff, you will ruff another diamond in the South hand for your tenth trick.

## DUCKING WHEN AN HONOR APPEARS

Another potential advantage of leading towards honor holdings is that you can duck (into the safe hand) when the safe defender follows in second seat with a high honor. Look at the diamond suit on this deal:

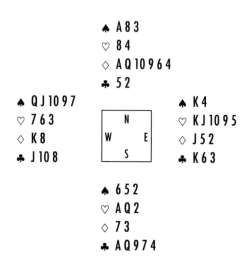

|       ♠ A 8 3       |
|       ♡ 8 4         |
|       ◊ A Q 10 9 6 4 |
|       ♣ 5 2         |

| WEST | NORTH | EAST | SOUTH |
|------|-------|------|-------|
|      | 1◊    | 1♡   | 2♣    |
| pass | 2◊    | pass | 3NT   |
| all pass |   |      |       |

South's 3NT may seem like an overbid, but he reasoned that his ♡A-Q, sitting over the ♡K, was worth 7 points rather than 6. West leads the ♠Q and East overtakes with the ♠K when you duck in the dummy. How will you play the contract when East returns the ♠4?

After the cards that you have seen, spades are surely 5-2 and you should win the second round of spades with the ace. You cross to your hand with a finesse of the ♡Q and lead a diamond, planning to finesse the ◊10. If West follows somnolently with the ◊8 on the first round, nothing will stop you from scoring five diamond tricks. Let's say that West is a competent performer and rises with the ◊K. It's a great defense! You cannot afford to duck this trick, because the danger hand (West) would be on lead and would cash three spade tricks. So, you win with dummy's ◊A. What now?

It is still possible that West began with ◊K-J-x and you could play for that chance. The bidding suggests that the ♣K will be onside, however, and a better chance is to play for East to hold ♣K-x-x, with the additional chance that the ◊J will fall doubleton from one hand or the other.

Your next move is a club towards your hand. If East rises with the ♣K, you duck. Let's assume that he plays low, however, and you win with the ♣Q. Ace and another club is no good now, because East will have the opportunity to unblock the ♣K under the ace. No, you must return to dummy with a diamond to the queen (failing to drop the ◊J) and lead another club towards your hand. Again, if East rises with the ♣K, you will duck. If he plays low a second time, you will win with the ♣A and play a third club, which East has to win. The safe hand will be on lead and you will score one spade, two hearts, two diamonds and four clubs.

Look back to Trick 2. Why was it right to win the second spade? If you fail to do so and West continues with a third round of spades, East can beat you by discarding the ♣K!

## DUCKING THE OPENING LEAD

When one defender rates to be a 'danger hand', it can pay to duck as early as Trick 1. Let's see a couple of examples of this technique.

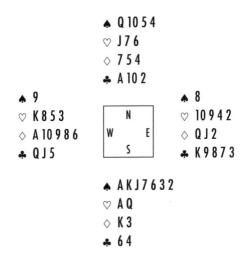

```
              ♠ Q 10 5 4
              ♡ J 7 6
              ◊ 7 5 4
              ♣ A 10 2
  ♠ 9                        ♠ 8
  ♡ K 8 5 3        N         ♡ 10 9 4 2
  ◊ A 10 9 8 6   W   E       ◊ Q J 2
  ♣ Q J 5          S         ♣ K 9 8 7 3
              ♠ A K J 7 6 3 2
              ♡ A Q
              ◊ K 3
              ♣ 6 4
```

| WEST | NORTH | EAST | SOUTH |
|------|-------|------|-------|
|      |       |      | 1♠    |
| pass | 2♠    | pass | 4♠    |
| all pass |   |      |       |

West leads the ♣Q against your spade game. How will you play the contract?

Let's see what happens if you win the opening lead with dummy's ♣A, East signalling enthusiasm with his ♣9. You draw both outstanding trumps with the ♠Q and finesse the ♡Q. The finesse loses and West leads the ♣5 to his partner's ♣K. Back comes the ◇Q and the defenders beat the contract by one trick.

East is the danger hand here, because he alone can lead diamonds effectively. So, you do what you can to keep him off lead. On this particular deal, you cannot prevent East from gaining the lead, but you can force him to pay too high a price for the privilege. You should play low at Trick 1, when the ♣Q is led. If East overtakes with the ♣K, dummy's ♣A-10 will be worth two tricks (via a finesse) and you will be able to ditch one of your red-suit losers. If East does not overtake, you win the club continuation, draw trumps and play a heart to the queen. The finesse loses, but the contract is secure. There is no entry to the East hand and when you regain the lead, you will be able to throw a loser on dummy's ♡J.

## Ducking into the safe hand

Suppose you hold A-10-4 opposite K-9-5-2 and need to develop a third trick from the suit without allowing a particular defender to gain the lead. It is a basic technique to lead low to the ten, or low to the nine, making sure that you duck into the safe hand.

Nothing 'unusual' about that, you might be thinking, so let's look at something a bit more advanced:

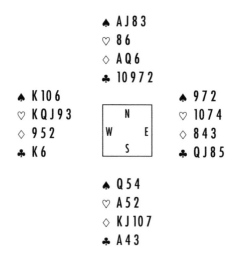

```
              ♠ A J 8 3
              ♡ 8 6
              ◇ A Q 6
              ♣ 10 9 7 2
♠ K 10 6                        ♠ 9 7 2
♡ K Q J 9 3      N              ♡ 10 7 4
◇ 9 5 2       W     E           ◇ 8 4 3
♣ K 6            S              ♣ Q J 8 5
              ♠ Q 5 4
              ♡ A 5 2
              ◇ K J 10 7
              ♣ A 4 3
```

| WEST | NORTH | EAST | SOUTH |
|------|-------|------|-------|
| 1♡ | pass | pass | 1NT |
| pass | 2♣ | pass | 2◇ |
| pass | 2NT | pass | 3NT |
| all pass | | | |

How will you play 3NT when West leads the ♡K?

Only 15 points are missing, so West is likely to hold the ♠K. A finesse of dummy's ♠J will give you eight tricks. Where can you seek a ninth? One chance is that West holds a doubleton ♠K. In that case, it will fall under dummy's ace, giving you three spade tricks. Is there a better chance?

You should hold up the ♡A until the third round, aiming to break the link between the defenders' hands. Next, you can make the avoidance play of a spade to the eight! East wins with the nine and has no heart to return. He will doubtless switch to a low club. You rise with the ace and play another spade. If West began with a doubleton king of spades, this card will now appear and you will score the three spade tricks that you need, despite your early finesse of the ♠8. The benefit comes when West holds three spades to the king. You finesse dummy's ♠J, cash the ♠A and eventually make the ♠3 as your ninth trick.

Suppose West finds an unlikely switch to the ♣K at Trick 3. You win the second round of clubs and have to develop spades without allowing East (now the danger hand, with a cashable club) to gain the lead. You finesse the ♠J and play ace and another spade. West, the safe hand, wins the third round of spades and the contract is again yours.

Only a top-class declarer would land the next contract. Step up to the plate and see if you make the grade.

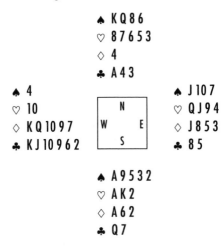

```
                    ♠ K Q 8 6
                    ♡ 8 7 6 5 3
                    ◇ 4
                    ♣ A 4 3
        ♠ 4                        ♠ J 10 7
        ♡ 10           N           ♡ Q J 9 4
        ◇ K Q 10 9 7  W   E        ◇ J 8 5 3
        ♣ K J 10 9 6 2    S        ♣ 8 5
                    ♠ A 9 5 3 2
                    ♡ A K 2
                    ◇ A 6 2
                    ♣ Q 7
```

| WEST | NORTH | EAST | SOUTH |
|------|-------|------|-------|
|      |       |      | 1♠    |
| 2NT  | 4◇    | pass | 4♡    |
| pass | 5♣    | pass | 6♠    |
| all pass |   |      |       |

West's Unusual Notrump overcall shows at least 5-5 shape in the minors and North's 4◇ is a splinter bid. Two cuebids later, you find yourself in a small slam. How will you play this when West leads the ♡10, East following with the ♡4?

You can ruff your two diamond losers and will have to set up dummy's hearts in order to dispose of your club loser. Let's suppose that you win the opening lead with the ♡A and pause to make a plan. Too late! With trumps breaking 3-1 and hearts 4-1, there is no way to make the contract. You can take the two diamond ruffs, but however you time the play, East will return a club when he takes his heart trick. With the ♣A removed, you will not be able to enjoy a long heart.

Since the chosen line of play will inevitably involve losing a round of hearts at some stage, you should arrange to do this when the defenders can inflict the least damage. You must, in fact, duck the ♡10 at Trick 1! West cannot safely dislodge the ♣A, because he would be leading away from the ♣K. He will probably switch to the ◇K. All is now easy. You win with the ace, ruff a diamond and cash the king and queen of trumps, West discarding a club on the second round. You then play the ace and king of hearts, re-enter dummy with your second diamond ruff and establish a long heart with a ruff. After drawing East's last trump, you cross to the ♣A and discard your club loser on the long heart. Slam made!

Note that East cannot afford to overtake the ♡10 at Trick 1. If he does that, you will win the trick and play the king and queen of trumps. You can then lead the ♡8, forcing East to split his remaining ♡J-9. It will then be a simple matter to set up two heart winners, on which you can discard one club and one diamond.

## DUCKING WHEN THE LOWEST SPOT CARD APPEARS

When the danger hand follows in the second seat with the lowest outstanding spot card, you can simply duck from the next hand to ensure that the safe defender wins the trick. West was asleep on the next deal, but declarer still needed to play sharply to take advantage.

```
                    ♠ K 7 6
                    ♡ Q 8 4
                    ◇ K 7 2
                    ♣ K 6 3 2
   ♠ 8 4                         ♠ Q J 9 5 2
   ♡ J 10 9 7 5     ┌─────────┐  ♡ 6 2
   ◇ Q J 8          │ N       │  ◇ A 10 9 5 3
   ♣ Q 9 7          │ W     E │  ♣ 10
                    │    S    │
                    └─────────┘
                    ♠ A 10 3
                    ♡ A K 3
                    ◇ 6 4
                    ♣ A J 8 5 4
```

| WEST | NORTH | EAST | SOUTH |
|------|-------|------|-------|
|      |       |      | 1NT   |
| pass | 3NT   | all pass |    |

A diamond lead would have hit the spot, but West began with the ♡J. Take the South cards now. How would you have played the contract?

You need to develop the club suit without allowing West, the danger hand, to gain the lead. All will be well when West holds fewer than three clubs. What can you do in the case where West holds three clubs?

A holding of ♣Q-10-9 will guarantee West an entry and leave you at the mercy of a diamond switch. Suppose West holds ♣Q-10-7 or ♣Q-9-7, though. The odds are good that he will follow nonchalantly with the ♣7 when you lead a low club from the South hand. Since this is the lowest spot card out, you can duck in the dummy! East, the safe hand, has to overtake with the ♣10 here and cannot attack diamonds effectively from his side of the table. You can win any return and score nine tricks.

If West had been fully awake, he would have played the ♣9 on the first round (also the ♣10 from ♣Q-10-7). It would then be rather dangerous for you to duck, because the West hand might gain the lead if he had started with ♣Q-9 or ♣10-9 or even a singleton ♣9. Rest assured that the defenders who would think of playing the middle card from these club combinations are few and far between!

## Avoidance play to prepare for a throw-in

On the next deal, an opening bid by one of the defenders makes it clear that you should aim for an endplay, rather than take either of the possible finesses. However, you must take special steps to prevent the other defender from gaining the lead as you prepare the end position.

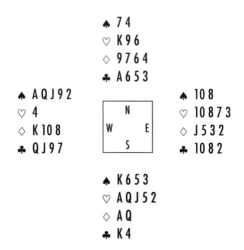

|  | ♠ 7 4 |  |
|  | ♡ K 9 6 |  |
|  | ◇ 9 7 6 4 |  |
|  | ♣ A 6 5 3 |  |

♠ A Q J 9 2  
♡ 4  
◇ K 10 8  
♣ Q J 9 7  

♠ 10 8  
♡ 10 8 7 3  
◇ J 5 3 2  
♣ 10 8 2  

♠ K 6 5 3  
♡ A Q J 5 2  
◇ A Q  
♣ K 4  

| WEST | NORTH | EAST | SOUTH |
|------|-------|------|-------|
| 1♠ | pass | pass | dbl |
| pass | 2♣ | pass | 2♡ |
| pass | 3♡ | pass | 3NT |
| all pass | | | |

Game in hearts would have gone down after a club (or a trump) lead. You went to bed early the previous night, however, and bid an inspired 3NT on the third round. How will you play this contract when West leads the ♣Q?

You must aim to throw in West with the fourth round of clubs at a time when he will have to return a spade or diamond, thereby giving you a ninth trick. Only one play is good enough — you must duck the first round of clubs to ensure that East (the danger hand, who can lead through your tenaces) does not gain the lead on the second or third round of the suit. Let's say that West continues with another club, which you win with the king.

You cash the ace, queen and king of hearts, removing West's holding in the suit. You then play ace and another club, discarding two spades from the South hand. West wins the trick and must surrender a trick by leading a spade or a diamond.

On the next deal, the avoidance play to prepare for a throw-in comes as early as Trick 2. Not the moment to be half asleep.

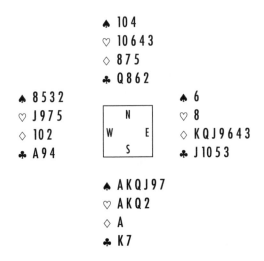

|  | ♠ 10 4 |  |
|  | ♡ 10 6 4 3 |  |
|  | ◇ 8 7 5 |  |
|  | ♣ Q 8 6 2 |  |
| ♠ 8 5 3 2 |  | ♠ 6 |
| ♡ J 9 7 5 |  | ♡ 8 |
| ◇ 10 2 |  | ◇ K Q J 9 6 4 3 |
| ♣ A 9 4 |  | ♣ J 10 5 3 |
|  | ♠ A K Q J 9 7 |  |
|  | ♡ A K Q 2 |  |
|  | ◇ A |  |
|  | ♣ K 7 |  |

| WEST | NORTH | EAST | SOUTH |
|------|-------|------|-------|
|  |  | 3◇ | dbl |
| pass | 3♡ | pass | 4NT |
| pass | 5♣ | pass | 6♠ |
| all pass |  |  |  |

You win the ◇10 lead with the ace. What is your plan for the contract?

There will be no problem if the ♡J falls in three rounds. When a defender, presumably West, holds ♡J-x-x-x, you must hope to endplay him with the ♣A. Perhaps you should draw trumps and test the heart suit? Let's hope not! It would then be much too late to set up the endplay you require.

At Trick 2, you must lead the ♣7. This is an avoidance play, through the ♣A that you expect and hope that West holds. If West rises with the ♣A, you will have two club tricks. Since you have not yet played a single round of trumps, you would be able to enjoy both the king and queen of clubs, even on a trump return from West.

Let's assume that West plays low on the first round of clubs. You win with dummy's ♣Q and draw trumps in four rounds. When you play the ace and king of hearts, East shows out on the second round. That's no problem now. Your careful play early in the deal is about to pay off. You run all your trumps, forcing West to abandon his heart guard or to reduce to ♡J-9 ♣A. You can then throw him in with a club to give you two heart tricks on the return.

A trump lead is rarely best against a small slam, but on this deal, it would have worked nicely. West would then have been able to rise with the ♣A and return a second trump to dummy's ten, while your club winners were blocked.

## AVOIDANCE PLAY IN THE TRUMP SUIT

When you have a two-way finesse against the queen of trumps, it a matter of basic technique to finesse into the safe hand — even sometimes when you are missing only four cards to the queen. Let's see something a little more difficult:

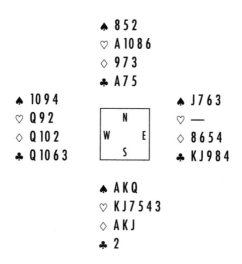

```
               ♠ 852
               ♡ A 10 8 6
               ◇ 973
               ♣ A 7 5
  ♠ 10 9 4                    ♠ J 7 6 3
  ♡ Q 9 2        N            ♡ —
  ◇ Q 10 2    W     E         ◇ 8 6 5 4
  ♣ Q 10 6 3      S           ♣ K J 9 8 4
               ♠ A K Q
               ♡ K J 7 5 4 3
               ◇ A K J
               ♣ 2
```

| WEST | NORTH | EAST | SOUTH |
|------|-------|------|-------|
|      |       |      | 2♣ |
| pass | 2◇ | pass | 2♡ |
| pass | 3♡ | pass | 4NT |
| pass | 5♡ | pass | 5♠ |
| pass | 6♡ | all pass | |

Roman Keycard Blackwood tells you that the ♡Q is missing, so you stop in the small slam. West leads the ♠10 and you win with the ♠A. What is your plan for the contract?

If you can pick up the trump suit without loss, your worries will be over. It is anyone's guess which defender is more likely to hold ♡Q-9-2. What play should you make on the next trick? (If you come up with the right answer, I will be forced to admit that you are a strong card player!)

If you play the ♡K next, or play a low card to the ♡A, you are relying on guesswork. In situations like this, you must ask yourself: if I guess wrongly, what remaining chance will there be? The answer on this deal is that there will be a considerable remaining chance if you play the ♡A first (and East shows out), providing you have paved the way for an elimination ending!

You should cross to the ♣A at Trick 2 and ruff a club. Only then do you play a trump to dummy's ace. If trumps break 2-1 or East turns up with all three trumps, you pick up the trumps without loss and make the slam easily. If instead East shows out, leaving you with a trump loser, you will ruff another club.

With the club suit eliminated, you cash the ♡K and continue with your remaining spade winners. You can then throw in West with the ♡Q, forcing him to lead a diamond into your tenace or concede a ruff-and-sluff. This line will fail only when West can overruff the second or third club, exit safely with his remaining trump and then score a diamond trick later.

Let's see one more deal where your play in the trump suit forms a big part of the main plan.

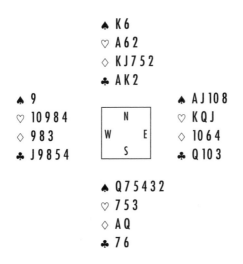

| WEST | NORTH | EAST | SOUTH |
|------|-------|------|-------|
|      | 1♢    | dbl  | 1♠    |
| pass | 2NT   | pass | 3♠    |
| pass | 4♠    | all pass |    |

How will you play the spade game when West leads the ♡10?

You win with dummy's ♡A and East produces the ♡J. Unless this is an unblocking maneuver from K-Q-J-x, East holds only three hearts and is therefore very likely indeed to hold four spades for his low point-count double. How will you continue?

You must turn to the diamond suit, with the intention of discarding a heart or two. You cash the ace and queen of diamonds and return to dummy with the ♣A. When you play the ◇K, discarding one of your heart losers, both defenders follow. What next?

It's not a good idea to play another diamond immediately. You can dispose of your last heart, yes, but West will ruff with his singleton spade. You will then lose a total of four trump tricks. You need to play one round of trumps before continuing diamonds. What's more, you must lead through East's ♠A, so that it will be too expensive for him to rise with the card.

'Six of trumps, please,' you say. What can East do? If he rises with the ♠A to cash a heart winner, you will lose only two trump tricks and one heart. If he plays low, you will win with the ♠Q, return to dummy with a club and only then play a fourth round of diamonds. You will discard your last heart on this trick, whatever happens. If East chooses to ruff, it will be from a natural trump trick. You will lose three trump tricks and no hearts, making your game exactly.

**1**

           ♠ 8 5
           ♡ A Q 7 6 5 2
           ◇ J 5 4
           ♣ A 8

♣K led

           ♠ K 6 4 3
           ♡ K 9
           ◇ A K Q 7
           ♣ 7 5 2

| WEST | NORTH | EAST | SOUTH |
|------|-------|------|-------|
|      |       |      | 1NT   |
| pass | 2◇    | pass | 2♡    |
| pass | 4♡    | all pass |   |

West leads the ♣K against your heart game. How will you proceed?

**2**

           ♠ 5 2
           ♡ A 7 3
           ◇ 10 8 7 3 2
           ♣ A Q 6

♠7 led

           ♠ K J 8
           ♡ K 8 4
           ◇ A K 4
           ♣ K 8 5 3

| WEST | NORTH | EAST | SOUTH |
|------|-------|------|-------|
|      |       |      | 1NT   |
| pass | 3NT   | all pass |   |

West leads the ♠7 against 3NT and East plays the ♠10. How will you play?

1

```
                    ♠ 8 5
                    ♡ A Q 7 6 5 2
                    ◇ J 5 4
                    ♣ A 8
    ♠ A Q 9 7                      ♠ J 10 2
    ♡ 10            ┌─────────┐    ♡ J 8 4 3
    ◇ 9 6 3 2       │ N       │    ◇ 10 8
    ♣ K Q J 4       │ W     E │    ♣ 10 9 6 4
                    │    S    │
                    └─────────┘
                    ♠ K 6 4 3
                    ♡ K 9
                    ◇ A K Q 7
                    ♣ 7 5 2
```

| WEST | NORTH | EAST | SOUTH |
|------|-------|------|-------|
|      |       |      | 1NT   |
| pass | 2◇    | pass | 2♡    |
| pass | 4♡    | all pass |    |

West leads the ♣K against your heart game. How will you proceed?

If the cards lie perfectly, you can make twelve tricks — six trumps, four diamonds and two black-suit winners. Suppose, however, you begin by playing the king and the ace of trumps. You will go down in game! East will gain the lead with a trump, ruffing the third diamond, and the defenders will add three tricks in the black suits.

You need to prevent East from gaining the lead and playing a spade through your king. In time, you will then be able to discard one of dummy's spades on the fourth round of diamonds. The first step is to allow the opening lead of the ♣K to hold the trick. Otherwise, there is a chance that West will be able to cross to the ♣J or ♣10 in the East hand. You win the club continuation and make a second avoidance play — a trump to your nine. This will prevent East from gaining the lead in trumps, unless he has an impregnable ♡J-10-x-x. West wins with the singleton ♡10, but cannot attack spades effectively from his side of the table. Nor, thanks to your hold-up at Trick 1, can he cross to the East hand with a club. On any return, you will be able to draw trumps in three further rounds and then discard one of dummy's spades on your diamond suit. You will score five trumps, four diamonds and the ♣A.

(2)

```
              ♠ 5 2
              ♡ A 7 3
              ◇ 10 8 7 3 2
              ♣ A Q 6
♠ A Q 9 7 3              ♠ 10 6 4
♡ Q 10 9 6      N       ♡ J 5 2
◇ J 5       W     E     ◇ Q 9 6
♣ 9 2           S       ♣ J 10 7 4
              ♠ K J 8
              ♡ K 8 4
              ◇ A K 4
              ♣ K 8 5 3
```

| WEST | NORTH | EAST | SOUTH |
|------|-------|------|-------|
|      |       |      | 1NT   |
| pass | 3NT   | all pass |   |

West leads the ♠7 against 3NT and East plays the ♠10. How will you play the contract?

You win with the ♠J and see that you have eight top tricks. A 3-3 club break will give you an easy ninth trick, but, with the deal appearing in a bridge book, you suspect that such a break is even less likely than normal. You must look for a way to set up the diamond suit without allowing East, the danger hand, to gain the lead. Can you see how to do this?

You must cross to the ♣Q and lead the ◇10 from dummy. (You could lead the ◇8 with the same effect.) If East fails to cover, you will duck the first round of diamonds into the safe West hand. West will not be able to continue spades effectively from his side of the table and you will have nine tricks when you regain the lead.

What happens if East covers the ◇10 with the ◇Q? You will win with the ◇A and return to dummy with a heart or a club. You can then lead the ◇8. East cannot afford to cover with the ◇9 or you will score all five diamond tricks. He plays low and you run the card to West, losing to the ◇J. As before, the diamond suit is established and the safe hand is on lead. The game is yours.

*Unusual Avoidance Play* 111

# CHAPTER 8

# SCORING THE LOW TRUMPS IN YOUR HAND

> *So high, so low*
> Ben Harper

At an early stage in your bridge education, you learn that taking a ruff in the short-trump hand (usually the dummy) will give you an extra trick. Most of the time, ruffing in the long-trump hand will not produce an extra trick. That's because you will be making a trump that would have scored a trick anyway.

Why is it, then, that you often see expert declarers taking an early ruff in their hand? One reason is that they wish to score a low trump that would not necessarily have been a winner in its own right. That is the case here:

```
              ♠ A J 8 5 2
              ♡ A 9 8 5
              ◇ 6 3 2
              ♣ 6
  ♠ 10 9 6                   ♠ K Q 7 4
  ♡ Q 10 6 3      N          ♡ K J
  ◇ K J       W     E        ◇ Q 10 9 7
  ♣ J 9 8 4       S          ♣ 10 5 3
              ♠ 3
              ♡ 7 4 2
              ◇ A 8 5 4
              ♣ A K Q 7 2
```

| WEST | NORTH | EAST | SOUTH |
|------|-------|------|-------|
|      |       |      | 1♣    |
| pass | 1♠    | pass | 2♣    |
| all pass |   |      |       |

You arrive in a contract where the defenders hold more trumps than you do. Suppose first that West leads the ♠10. How will you tackle the play?

Your general aim should be to score the two low trumps in your hand, by ruffing spades. This is easy on a spade lead. You win with the ace, ruff a spade and cash the ace-king-queen of trumps, both defenders following all the way. You then cross to the ace of hearts and ruff another spade with your last trump. You score five trump tricks and three aces.

Now suppose that West finds the more inspired lead of the ♡3. Not so easy now, is it? The defenders are threatening to remove dummy's ♡A before you are ready to use it. You play low on the first heart and East wins with the king. When he returns the ♡J, you must allow this to win too! West cannot afford to overtake with the queen of hearts or you would win with the ace and score a trick from dummy's ♡9-8. East has no further heart to play and the defenders have no way to dislodge the ace of hearts. You win East's diamond switch and draw three rounds of trumps. You can then cross to the ace of spades, ruff a spade, cross to the heart ace and ruff another spade. If East held the last trump and could ruff the ace of hearts, you would still survive if diamonds were 3-3.

## SCORING THE LOW TRUMPS TO SURVIVE A BAD TRUMP BREAK

Sometimes you must make full use of every entry to dummy. You may, for example, have to take a ruff in your hand at Trick 2, just in case this proves necessary later (when a bad trump break comes to light). Let's see an example of this.

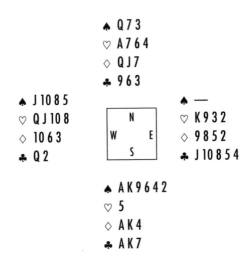

| WEST | NORTH | EAST | SOUTH |
|------|-------|------|-------|
|      |       |      | 1♠    |
| pass | 2♠    | pass | 6♠    |
| all pass |   |      |       |

If this were a book on bidding, the auction here might cause you to ask for your money back. No refund, sorry. This is a book on play. How will you tackle the small slam when West leads the ♡Q, won with dummy's ace?

You have twelve top tricks, unless trumps break 4-0. So, you should address this possibility immediately. How can you make the slam when one of the defenders holds four trumps?

The first point to make is that you can pick up ♠J-10-8-5 with East directly, provided you cash the queen on the first round of trumps. If West shows out, you will lead a trump towards your hand, intending to finesse the ♠9. East will no doubt split his trump honors, but you can return to dummy with a diamond to pick up the outstanding trumps.

What can you do if it is West who holds four trumps, as in the diagram? You will have to score six trump tricks in the South hand (by ruffing three hearts) and add six side-suit winners to bring the total to twelve. You must take the first of the necessary heart ruffs in your hand now, at Trick 2, even though you have no reason to suspect that West will hold four trumps.

You ruff a heart in your hand and cross to the queen of trumps. East shows out on this trick and you take advantage of the dummy entry to ruff another heart. A diamond to the queen allows you to ruff dummy's last heart. West follows suit when you cash the two minor-suit ace-kings and the ♠K brings in your twelfth trick. At Trick 13, you lead the ♣7 and West has to ruff his partner's club winner, condensing two defensive tricks into one. Enjoy the moment!

When the adverse trump holding lies in front of your own long trumps, you can often work miracles. That's because the defender has less potential for ruffing with his intermediate trumps. If he does, you will simply discard a loser.

                    ♠ K Q 7 5
                    ♡ A K 7 6 4
                    ◇ J 6
                    ♣ A 6

    ♠ —                              ♠ J 10 9 6
    ♡ Q 9 8 3        ┌─────────┐     ♡ J 5
    ◇ Q 8 2         │ N       │     ◇ 10 7 5 4
    ♣ K Q 10 8 5 3  │ W   E   │     ♣ J 9 4
                    │    S    │
                    └─────────┘
                    ♠ A 8 4 3 2
                    ♡ 10 2
                    ◇ A K 9 3
                    ♣ 7 2

| WEST | NORTH | EAST | SOUTH |
|------|-------|------|-------|
|      |       |      | 1♠    |
| 2♣   | 3♣    | pass | 3◇    |
| pass | 4NT   | pass | 5♡    |
| pass | 6♠    | all pass |   |

You win the ♣K lead in the dummy and play the ♠K, discovering how unfair the world can be when West shows out. How will you attempt to recover the situation?

With a certain trump loser looming, you must somehow dispose of your club loser. You will need to establish dummy's heart suit. You cash the ace and king of hearts and the jack falls on your right. What can East do when you continue with another heart from dummy?

If East ruffs from his ♠J-10-9, you can discard your club loser and easily score the balance. If instead East throws a diamond, you can establish the diamond suit with one ruff, return to hand with a heart ruff and play the good diamond, throwing dummy's club. So, let's assume that East discards a club on the third round of hearts. You ruff cheaply, cash the two top diamonds and ruff a diamond in dummy. When you lead a fourth round of hearts from the table, East is again without resource. Let's say he throws his last club. You score yet another low trump in your hand, ruff another diamond in dummy and score the queen and ace of trumps, conceding the last trick.

What tricks did you make on that line of play? Five winners in the side suits, two diamond ruffs in dummy, two heart ruffs with low trumps in your hand, plus the ace, king and queen of trumps.

## Scoring the low trumps to prepare for a trump coup

Sometimes the action of scoring the low trumps in your hand will lead to the end position known as a 'trump coup'. That's what happens on this deal:

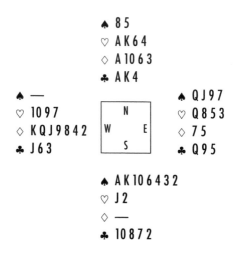

```
                    ♠ 8 5
                    ♡ A K 6 4
                    ◇ A 10 6 3
                    ♣ A K 4
    ♠ —                           ♠ Q J 9 7
    ♡ 10 9 7           N          ♡ Q 8 5 3
    ◇ K Q J 9 8 4 2  W   E        ◇ 7 5
    ♣ J 6 3            S          ♣ Q 9 5
                    ♠ A K 10 6 4 3 2
                    ♡ J 2
                    ◇ —
                    ♣ 10 8 7 2
```

| WEST | NORTH | EAST | SOUTH |
|------|-------|------|-------|
| 3◇ | 3NT | pass | 5♠ |
| pass | 6♠ | all pass | |

With no scientific route available, South invites a slam by leaping to 5♠. North accepts the invitation and the ◇K is led. How will you play the contract?

You win the diamond lead in dummy, ditching a club. You have five side-suit winners and will make the slam if you can add seven trump tricks. You ruff a diamond at Trick 2 and cash the ♠A, hoping for a 2-2 trump break. Not today, as West discards a diamond on the first round of trumps. How will you continue?

You have a wealth of entries to dummy and should continue to score your low trumps. You cross to the ♡A and lead a third round of diamonds. (East cannot damage you by ruffing. If he ruffs with the ♠9, you will overruff with the ♠10 and continue to ruff cards in your hand, eventually promoting your last trump *en passant*. If instead East ruffs with the ♠J, you will discard your last club loser, win the return and pick up East's remaining ♠Q-9 with a straight finesse.) So, let's assume that East discards a club and you ruff the third round of diamonds in your hand.

A heart to the king is followed by a heart ruff in your hand. You can then return to dummy with the ♣A to ruff dummy's last heart. Having taken four ruffs in your hand so far, you return to dummy once more with the ♣K. These cards are still to be played:

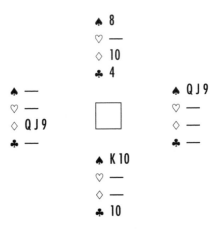

```
              ♠ 8
              ♡ —
              ◇ 10
              ♣ 4
  ♠ —                      ♠ Q J 9
  ♡ —                      ♡ —
  ◇ Q J 9     ┌─────┐      ◇ —
  ♣ —         │     │      ♣ —
              └─────┘
              ♠ K 10
              ♡ —
              ◇ —
              ♣ 10
```

You lead dummy's ◇10 and East cannot prevent you from scoring your ♠10. If he ruffs with the ♠Q or the ♠J, you will discard the ♣10 and finesse on his obligatory trump return.

The play may have looked smooth as it was being described. There was, in fact, a pitfall to be avoided. If you took a third diamond ruff too early, East would have had the chance to discard the second of his three clubs. If you had not used both of the club entries by this stage, you would have had to wave goodbye to one of your club winners. By ruffing the two hearts before the final diamond, you prevented East from making a damaging discard.

Let's see one more example of this style of play:

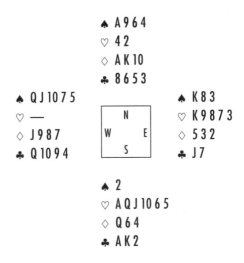

```
                    ♠ A 9 6 4
                    ♡ 4 2
                    ◇ A K 10
                    ♣ 8 6 5 3
  ♠ Q J 10 7 5                      ♠ K 8 3
  ♡ —            ┌─────────┐        ♡ K 9 8 7 3
  ◇ J 9 8 7      │ N       │        ◇ 5 3 2
  ♣ Q 10 9 4     │ W     E │        ♣ J 7
                 │    S    │
                 └─────────┘
                    ♠ 2
                    ♡ A Q J 10 6 5
                    ◇ Q 6 4
                    ♣ A K 2
```

| WEST | NORTH | EAST | SOUTH |
|------|-------|------|-------|
|      |       |      | 1♡    |
| pass | 1♠    | pass | 4♡    |
| pass | 6♡    | all pass |   |

"Even at our club they don't bid as badly as that!" you must be thinking. I believe you. But, of course, this is a book on card play and no complaints about the bidding are allowed. West leads the ♠Q and you win with dummy's ace. A trump to the queen brings good news and bad news. The finesse wins, but West throws a spade. How will you continue?

Your general plan is to finesse the ♡J, score the ♡6 and the ♡5 by ruffing spades and then to exit, making the last two tricks with your ♡A-10. Since this requires three further entries to dummy, you must steel yourself to finesse dummy's ◊10. Fortune favors the brave and the diamond finesse wins. You continue with a trump to East's ♡7 and your ♡J. You cash your top two clubs and re-enter dummy twice in diamonds to ruff two spades with low trumps. These cards remain:

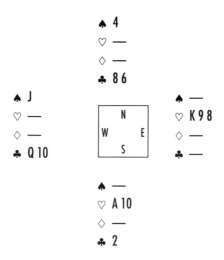

There is no need to lead a plain card from dummy towards your trump tenace. You simply exit with the ♣2. East has to ruff and lead a trump. The slam is yours.

**1**

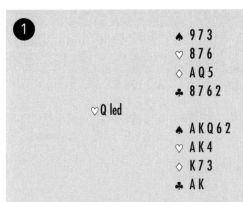

♠ 9 7 3
♡ 8 7 6
◇ A Q 5
♣ 8 7 6 2

♡ Q led

♠ A K Q 6 2
♡ A K 4
◇ K 7 3
♣ A K

You arrive in 6♠, played by South, and West leads the ♡Q. You win in your hand and play two top trumps, not overjoyed to see West discarding a diamond on the second round. How will you continue?

**2**

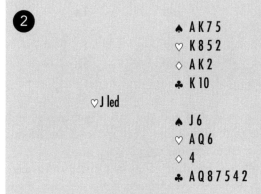

♠ A K 7 5
♡ K 8 5 2
◇ A K 2
♣ K 10

♡ J led

♠ J 6
♡ A Q 6
◇ 4
♣ A Q 8 7 5 4 2

Bidding with your usual flair, you reach the fine contract of 7♣. You win the ♡J lead in your hand and play a low trump towards dummy, preparing to claim the contract. Not so fast! West discards a diamond on the first round of trumps. So, East began with ♣J-9-6-3. What is your plan to make the grand slam, preventing East from scoring a trump trick?

1

```
                  ♠ 9 7 3
                  ♡ 8 7 6
                  ◊ A Q 5
                  ♣ 8 7 6 2
   ♠ 4                           ♠ J 10 8 5
   ♡ Q J 10 5      ┌─────────┐   ♡ 9 3 2
   ◊ 9 8 4 2       │    N    │   ◊ J 10 6
   ♣ J 10 4 3      │ W     E │   ♣ Q 9 5
                   │    S    │
                   └─────────┘
                  ♠ A K Q 6 2
                  ♡ A K 4
                  ◊ K 7 3
                  ♣ A K
```

| WEST | NORTH | EAST | SOUTH |
|------|-------|------|-------|
|      |       |      | 2♣ |
| pass | 2◊ | pass | 2♠ |
| pass | 3♠ | pass | 4♣ |
| pass | 4◊ | pass | 4♡ |
| pass | 4♠ | pass | 6♠ |
| all pass | | | |

West leads the ♡Q against your slam and you win in the South hand. Everything will be easy if trumps break 3-2, but when you cash the ace and king of trumps, West shows out on the second round. What now?

It may seem that you have two unavoidable losers — a trump and a heart. Look at it another way, though. You have seven winners in the side suits. If you can score all five trumps in your hand, that will add up to twelve.

You might as well play another top trump before continuing with your other heart winner and the two top clubs. Next you play the king and the ace of diamonds. The time has come to score one of your two low trumps. You lead a club from dummy and ruff with the ♠2. You return to dummy with the ◊Q, East following suit, and are now guaranteed to make the contract. The last two cards in your hand are the ♠6 and the ♡4 (the two losers that you might have thought were unavoidable). You lead another club from dummy and East cannot defend the position. If he ruffs with his master trump, you will discard your heart loser and then score the promoted ♠6. If East discards, of course, you will ruff with the ♠6.

```
                    ♠ A K 7 5
                    ♡ K 8 5 2
                    ◇ A K 2
                    ♣ K 10
    ♠ Q 10 3                        ♠ 9 8 4 2
    ♡ J 10 9 3        N             ♡ 7 4
    ◇ J 9 8 6 5 3  W     E          ◇ Q 10 7
    ♣ —               S             ♣ J 9 6 3
                    ♠ J 6
                    ♡ A Q 6
                    ◇ 4
                    ♣ A Q 8 7 5 4 2
```

| WEST | NORTH | EAST | SOUTH |
|------|-------|------|-------|
|      |       |      | 1♣ |
| pass | 1♡ | pass | 3♣ |
| pass | 4NT | pass | 5♠ |
| pass | 7♣ | all pass | |

North's 4NT was Roman Keycard Blackwood and the 5♠ response showed two aces and the queen of trumps. West leads the ♡J, won with the ♡Q, and West discards a diamond when you lead a trump towards dummy. How will you attempt to overcome the 4-0 trump break?

You win with dummy's ♣K and lead the ♣10, covered by the jack and the ace. In order to pick up East's remaining ♣9-6, you must now shorten your trumps three times and then return to dummy to lead a plain card through East's trump holding at Trick 12. East will need to hold at least two spades (so that dummy's ace and king can provide you with two entries). He does not need to hold three hearts, however.

You play a diamond to the ace and continue with the ◇K, throwing your ♡A. You then ruff dummy's last diamond, cross to the ♡K and ruff a heart, East showing out. A spade to the ace is followed by a second heart ruff and you then return to dummy at Trick 11 with the ♠K. The hard work has been done. Your last two cards are the ♣Q-8, poised over East's ♣9-6. You lead a spade from dummy and make the grand slam, overruffing the trump that East chooses to play.

Look back at the tricks that you made: seven trump tricks and two winners in each of the side suits.

# CHAPTER 9

# LEAVING THE HIGHWAY

*Car wheels on a gravel road*
Lucinda Williams

One of the hardest things to do, for some reason, is to switch plans in the middle of a deal. This can become necessary when the fall of the cards tells you that your original plan will fail. Sometimes it's just that the play so far suggests that a different line will have a greater chance of success. There is no particular pattern to the deals in this chapter, except that at some point you should abandon one plan and switch to another. See how you fare!

```
                    ♠ A K 5
                    ♡ Q 6 3
                    ◇ 9 5 2
                    ♣ A K 10 4
      ♠ 8 4                          ♠ 9 3 2
      ♡ 10 7          N              ♡ A K J 8 4 2
      ◇ A J 10 7 4  W   E            ◇ 8 3
      ♣ J 9 8 5        S             ♣ 6 2
                    ♠ Q J 10 7 6
                    ♡ 9 5
                    ◇ K Q 6
                    ♣ Q 7 3
```

| WEST | NORTH | EAST | SOUTH |
|------|-------|------|-------|
|      | 1NT   | 2♡   | 3♠    |
| pass | 4♠    | all pass |    |

West leads the ♡10 against your spade game. East overtakes with the ♡J and continues with the ace and king of hearts. How will you play the contract?

First, let's see what happened when the deal occurred at the table. Declarer ruffed the third round of hearts high and drew trumps in three rounds, ending in the dummy. Expecting East to hold the ◇A because of his bid, declarer then played a diamond to the king.

The player in the West seat was a skilled defender. He realized that South must hold close to 10 points to force to game with only a five-card trump suit. That placed South with both the king and the queen of diamonds. West therefore followed smoothly with a low diamond, allowing South's ◇K to win.

Still assuming that the ◇A was onside, declarer cashed three rounds of clubs, just in case the ♣J would fall. When it didn't, he played a diamond towards the queen. West won with the ace and the game was one down.

Do you see why declarer should have avoided the trap that West set for him? East had shown up with three trumps and six hearts. If he did indeed hold the ◇A, along with the ◇3 that had already been played, he would have had room for no more than two clubs! So, declarer should have switched to a different track — playing the ace and queen of clubs and then finessing the ♣10.

(The recommended line of play would fail when East's minor-suit holdings were ◇3 and ♣J-x-x. In that case, he would surely have switched to his singleton diamond at Trick 3, rather than playing for an unlikely trump promotion.)

On the next deal, you must look for a way to test the trump situation before committing yourself to a particular line of play.

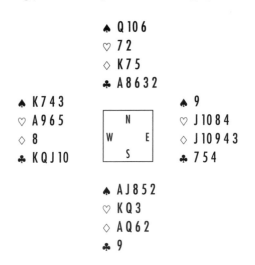

♠ Q 10 6
♡ 7 2
◇ K 7 5
♣ A 8 6 3 2

♠ K 7 4 3
♡ A 9 6 5
◇ 8
♣ K Q J 10

♠ 9
♡ J 10 8 4
◇ J 10 9 4 3
♣ 7 5 4

♠ A J 8 5 2
♡ K Q 3
◇ A Q 6 2
♣ 9

| WEST | NORTH | EAST | SOUTH |
| --- | --- | --- | --- |
| 1♣ | pass | pass | dbl |
| pass | 1NT | pass | 2♠ |
| pass | 4♠ | all pass | |

West leads the ♣K and you win with dummy's ♣A. The best initial plan is to score a heart ruff in dummy and then to draw trumps. When you play a heart to the king, West wins with the ace and forces you in clubs. How would you continue from this point?

Suppose you cash the ♡Q and ruff a heart in dummy. If your next move is to run the trump queen, you will go down. West will win with the king and force you again in clubs. You will have one trump fewer than he does and will lose a trump and a club trick for down one. There is no hurry to take a heart ruff. At Trick 4, you do better to lead a low trump from your hand instead of continuing hearts.

Let's assume that West jumps in with the ♠K and forces you again in clubs. You now have two trumps in each hand, while (unknown to you) West has three trumps. To discover the trump break, you lead the jack of trumps to dummy's queen. (If trumps were 3-2, you would take your intended heart ruff and return to a diamond honor to draw the last trump.) When the 4-1 trump break comes to light, you switch tracks. Now you ruff a fourth round of clubs yourself, with the ace, and cross to a diamond honor to draw West's penultimate trump. You continue with dummy's good club, throwing your potential diamond loser, after which you simply play red-suit winners, letting West score his trump whenever he pleases.

Next, we will look at some deals where you can acquire a count of all four hands. This will lead you to the conclusion that you should leave the road and strike out cross-country. Try this one:

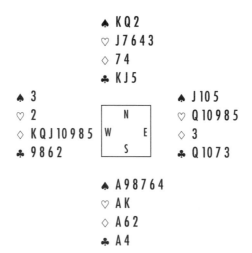

```
                    ♠ K Q 2
                    ♡ J 7 6 4 3
                    ◇ 7 4
                    ♣ K J 5
   ♠ 3                              ♠ J 10 5
   ♡ 2                  N           ♡ Q 10 9 8 5
   ◇ K Q J 10 9 8 5   W   E         ◇ 3
   ♣ 9 8 6 2              S         ♣ Q 10 7 3

                    ♠ A 9 8 7 6 4
                    ♡ A K
                    ◇ A 6 2
                    ♣ A 4
```

| WEST | NORTH | EAST | SOUTH |
|------|-------|------|-------|
|      |       |      | 1♠    |
| 4♦   | 4♠    | pass | 6♠    |
| all pass |    |      |       |

You save time by leaping directly to 6♠ and West leads the ◇K, East following. What's your plan?

There are eleven top tricks, assuming that the trumps are not 4-0, and one possible line of play is to set up a long heart. You could cash the trump ace, followed by two top hearts. If both defenders followed, you would cross to the trump king, ruff a heart, cross to the queen of trumps and ruff another heart. The ♣K would then serve as an entry to the long heart.

An alternative line is to draw two rounds of trumps straight away. If trumps break 2-2, a diamond ruff in dummy will give you a twelfth trick. If trumps break 3-1, you will still have the entries to set up and enjoy the hearts if that suit breaks 3-3. There will also be the club finesse as a final chance.

Suppose you embark on this second line. You win the diamond lead and play the king and ace of trumps, West discarding on the second round. When you cash the ace-king of hearts, West again shows out on the second round. Your plans to establish the suit have to be abandoned. Has the time come to take the club finesse? A better idea is to claim the contract! You know that East's shape is 3-5-1-4. So, you can endplay him with a heart. You cash the ♣A and cross to dummy with a third round of trumps. These cards remain:

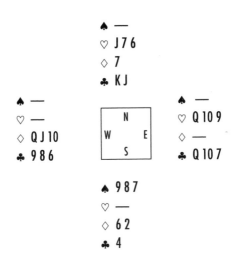

You put East on lead with a low heart, discarding a diamond from the South hand. Whether East returns a heart or a club, you will have twelve tricks.

On the next deal, an initial glance at the North-South hands reveals only one line of play, a finesse against the ◇J. Dig a little deeper and you will find that this finesse is against the odds. Perhaps you will hear the sound of gravel under your tires as another road appears.

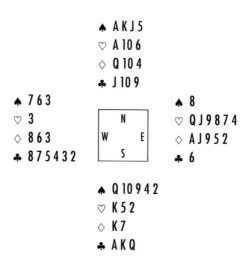

♠ A K J 5
♡ A 10 6
◇ Q 10 4
♣ J 10 9

♠ 7 6 3
♡ 3
◇ 8 6 3
♣ 8 7 5 4 3 2

♠ 8
♡ Q J 9 8 7 4
◇ A J 9 5 2
♣ 6

♠ Q 10 9 4 2
♡ K 5 2
◇ K 7
♣ A K Q

| WEST | NORTH | EAST | SOUTH |
|------|-------|------|-------|
|  | 1NT | 2♡ | 3♠ |
| pass | 4♡ | pass | 4NT |
| pass | 5♣ | pass | 6♠ |
| all pass |  |  |  |

West leads the ♡3 against your spade slam and you win in your hand with the ♡K. You then draw trumps, noting that East began with one card in the suit. At this point, only one line of play suggests itself — a finesse of the ◇10 to set up a discard for your heart loser. (As a small point of technique, you should lead the first round of diamonds from dummy, so that you do not suffer the indignity of losing two diamond tricks to the ◇A-J doubleton with East!) However, it costs you nothing to investigate the club position before playing diamonds. When you do so, East discards a heart on the second round.

It is time to re-assess the position. East's shape is 1-6-5-1. You can assume from his overcall that he holds the ◇A. That leaves four more Vacant Spaces in diamonds to accommodate the ◇J. West has only three Vacant Spaces for diamonds, so East is the favorite to hold that card. How can you make the contract if East does indeed hold the ◇J?

You cash your remaining club honor and then play your last two trumps. This will be the position as you lead your final trump:

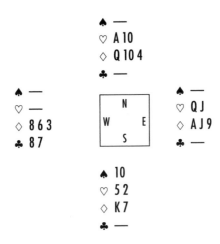

You lead the ♠10 and throw the ♡10 from dummy. East has no good discard. If he throws a heart, you will cross to the ♡A and lead towards the ◇K, setting up an entry to the established ♡5. If instead he throws the ◇9, you will lead the ◇K to his ◇A and subsequently drop the ◇J. After this display of wizardry, it would be unfair indeed to find yourself going down because the ◇J was onside all along!

On the next deal, West has advertised length in one suit and is likely to be short in another suit. When this proves not to be the case, you can switch tracks.

```
                    ♠ J 10 5 2
                    ♡ A K 8 6
                    ◇ A K 9
                    ♣ 9 3
    ♠ 3                             ♠ 9 7 6 4
    ♡ Q J 10 9 7 5    ┌─────┐      ♡ 2
    ◇ Q 7          W  │  N  │  E   ◇ J 10 8 4 3 2
    ♣ Q J 6 2         │  S  │      ♣ 8 5
                      └─────┘
                    ♠ A K Q 8
                    ♡ 4 3
                    ◇ 6 5
                    ♣ A K 10 7 4
```

| WEST | NORTH | EAST | SOUTH |
|------|-------|------|-------|
|      |       |      | 1♣    |
| 2♡   | dbl   | pass | 4♠    |
| pass | 4NT   | pass | 5♣    |
| pass | 5◇    | pass | 6♣    |
| pass | 7♠    | all pass |   |

North's 5◇ bid is part of Roman Keycard Blackwood and asks about the queen of trumps. South's 6♣ response says: 'Yes, I have the trump queen and also the ♣K.' How will you play the grand slam when West leads the ♡Q?

You must establish the clubs. Since West has six hearts to his partner's one, you half-expect him to hold a doubleton club. If that's the case, it will be easy to ruff two clubs in dummy. You will win the heart lead and cash the ♣A-K, both defenders following. When you lead a third round, West produces the ♣Q. What now?

If clubs are breaking 3-3, you can afford to ruff high, so you decide to ruff with the ♠J. East surprises you by showing out, discarding a diamond. You return to your hand with the ♠A and lead a fourth round of clubs. You have to ruff this with the ♠10 to avoid an overruff. The lead is in dummy and these cards remain:

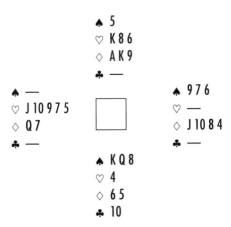

With West long in clubs as well as hearts, you must decide whether to finesse the ♠8 or not. How would you go about making your choice?

You must count the possible layouts where a finesse will gain and those where it will lose. It will gain when West has any remaining doubleton in diamonds. That is 15 possible cases. A finesse of the ♠8 will fail when West has the singleton ♠9 remaining and any singleton diamond (6 cases) or any remaining doubleton ♠9 (2 cases). So, the odds are almost 2-to-1 in favor of finessing the ♠8.

Moving swiftly on, what do you make of this deal?

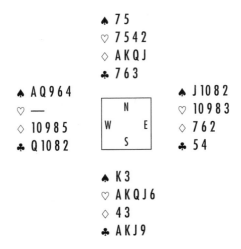

| WEST | NORTH | EAST | SOUTH |
|------|-------|------|-------|
|      |       |      | 1♡    |
| 1♠   | 2♠    | 3♠   | 4NT   |
| pass | 5♢    | pass | 6♡    |
| all pass |   |      |       |

West leads the ♢10 against your small slam and you win in the dummy, East playing the ♢2. The contract is an excellent one. Unless trumps break 4-0, you will be able to discard both your spades on the surplus diamond winners and ruff your potential fourth-round club loser in the dummy. When you play a trump to the ace, however, West discards a spade. What now?

Prospects are still fairly good. You could draw trumps, cash the ace-king of clubs and then run three more diamond winners, throwing both your spades. Finally, you could lead a third round of clubs towards your ♣J-9, losing only when West began with ♣Q-10-x-x. However, the East-West bidding should give you some concern about this line. East's somewhat unwise raise in spades tells you that spades are breaking 5-4. West has shown a void in hearts and there is a fair chance that his shape will be 5-0-4-4. This lie of the cards is made even more likely by East's count signal of the ♢2 at Trick 1. You don't like to rely on the defenders' signals, I dare say, but it is foolish to ignore them completely.

You draw the remaining trumps and West discards two more spades and a diamond. If West does indeed hold four clubs, there is no benefit in cashing the ♣A-K. The contract will be an easy make, anyway, if East's doubleton contains the queen or the ten. You will continue with two more diamond winners, discarding the ♠3. Both defenders follow all the way in diamonds, confirming your provisional count of the West hand as 5-0-4-4. You are about to play the last diamond winner, throwing the ♠K, when it occurs to you that the end position is something like this:

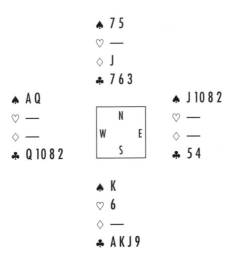

```
              ♠ 7 5
              ♡ —
              ◇ J
              ♣ 7 6 3
♠ A Q                    ♠ J 10 8 2
♡ —         ┌─────────┐  ♡ —
◇ —         │  N      │  ◇ —
♣ Q 10 8 2  │ W     E │  ♣ 5 4
            │     S   │
            └─────────┘
              ♠ K
              ♡ 6
              ◇ —
              ♣ A K J 9
```

West has two spade winners and four clubs. It is time to switch tracks. You cash dummy's last diamond winner and discard the ♣9. If West discards the ♠Q, you will endplay him with a spade to lead into your club tenace, so he has to throw a club. You cross to your hand with the ♣A and cash the last trump. West has no good discard. To retain his club guard, he has to discard the ♠Q. You then throw him in with the ♠A, forcing him to lead back into your club tenace.

On the next deal, the seemingly obvious line of play is made less likely to succeed by an effective start to the defense.

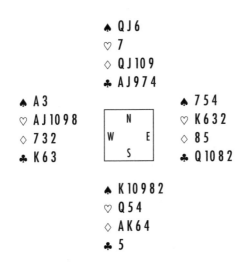

```
              ♠ Q J 6
              ♡ 7
              ◇ Q J 10 9
              ♣ A J 9 7 4
♠ A 3                    ♠ 7 5 4
♡ A J 10 9 8 ┌─────────┐ ♡ K 6 3 2
◇ 7 3 2      │  N      │ ◇ 8 5
♣ K 6 3      │ W     E │ ♣ Q 10 8 2
             │     S   │
             └─────────┘
              ♠ K 10 9 8 2
              ♡ Q 5 4
              ◇ A K 6 4
              ♣ 5
```

| WEST | NORTH | EAST | SOUTH |
|------|-------|------|-------|
|      |       |      | 1♠    |
| 2♡   | 3♣    | 3♡   | pass  |
| pass | 4♠    | all pass |   |

You can expect to make four trump tricks, four diamonds and the ♣A. A single heart ruff in the dummy will then bring the total to ten tricks. When the deal originally occurred, however, West found the defense of ace and another trump. How would you play the contract then?

The original declarer won the second round of trumps in dummy and led the ♡7, hoping that he might still be able to score a heart ruff. Not against the present defenders! East rose smartly with the ♡K and played a third round of trumps. No heart ruff was available, nor was there any catch-up route to ten tricks. The game went down one.

It was hardly likely that the defenders would permit a heart ruff after their bright start. Declarer should have switched tracks, aiming to set up dummy's club suit instead. After winning the second round of trumps, he should play a club to the ace and ruff a club. A diamond to the queen permits a second club ruff. Declarer then crosses to the jack of diamonds and ruffs yet another club, setting up a long card in the suit. These cards remain:

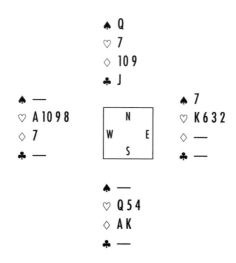

Declarer, who has already scored seven tricks, continues with the ace and king of diamonds. If East refuses to ruff, the total will be up to nine and dummy's ♠Q will be the tenth trick. If instead East ruffs one of the diamonds, a heart ruff will be the entry to reach the established ♣J.

The next deal, which closes the chapter, is somewhat different from the rest. The declarer saw only one road at his disposal, headed in that direction, but failed to reach the finish line. Had he played the hand to better effect, another track would have appeared. See what you make of it.

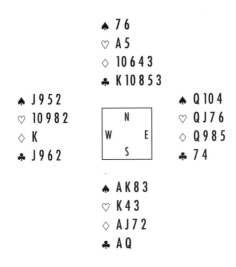

| WEST | NORTH | EAST | SOUTH |
|------|-------|------|-------|
|      |       |      | 2NT   |
| pass | 3NT   | all pass |   |

West leads the ♡10 against 3NT. How will you play the contract?

The original declarer won with the ♡K and studied the club suit. Suppose he cashed the ace and queen of clubs and crossed to the ♡A to play the ♣K. He would make the contract with an overtrick when clubs broke 3-3 or when the ♣J fell on the first two rounds. However, better odds could be achieved by overtaking the ♣Q on the second round. He would still make the four club tricks needed for the contract when clubs were 3-3 or the ♣J fell. He would also succeed when the ♣9 fell in two rounds and dummy's ♣10-8 were sufficient to drive out the ♣J.

Pleased with his analysis, declarer cashed the ♣A and overtook the ♣Q with the ♣K. No card of interest fell on the first two rounds. When he played a third round of clubs, the suit failed to break 3-3 and the contract went down.

Declarer took the best line in clubs, yes, but he failed to spot an extra chance. It costs nothing to cash the ◇A before playing the club suit. If an honor happens to fall on the first round, you can switch tracks. Knowing that three club tricks will suffice, you cash the ace and queen of the suit. You can then lead a second round of diamonds to establish an extra trick from that suit. You make the game by scoring two spades, two hearts, two diamonds and three clubs.

**1**

```
                    ♠ Q 9 3
                    ♡ Q J 10 2
                    ◇ 8 6 3 2
                    ♣ 4 2
    ♣ J led

                    ♠ A K J 10 8 5 4
                    ♡ —
                    ◇ A K J 5
                    ♣ A K
```

| WEST | NORTH | EAST | SOUTH |
|------|-------|------|-------|
| | | | 2♣ |
| pass | 2◇ | pass | 2♠ |
| pass | 4♠ | pass | 6♠ |
| all pass | | | |

How will you play 6♠ when West leads the ♣J? (Trumps will break 2-1.)

**2**

```
                    ♠ 3 2
                    ♡ 9 8 7 6
                    ◇ Q J 7 4
                    ♣ 7 5 2
    ♠ 6 led

                    ♠ A K 8
                    ♡ A K Q 10 4 3
                    ◇ A
                    ♣ A Q 4
```

| WEST | NORTH | EAST | SOUTH |
|------|-------|------|-------|
| | | | 2♣ |
| pass | 2◇ | pass | 2♡ |
| pass | 4♡ | pass | 6♡ |
| all pass | | | |

You win the spade lead and draw trumps, finding that West was void in the suit. How will you try to avoid two club losers? (If you take a spade ruff, you will find that West began with two spades.)

1

```
                    ♠ Q 9 3
                    ♡ Q J 10 2
                    ◇ 8 6 3 2
                    ♣ 4 2
   ♠ 7                              ♠ 6 2
   ♡ 9 7 5 4         ┌─────────┐    ♡ A K 8 6 3
   ◇ Q 10 9 4        │   N     │    ◇ 7
   ♣ J 10 9 7     W  │ W     E │  E ♣ Q 8 6 5 3
                     │     S   │
                     └─────────┘
                    ♠ A K J 10 8 5 4
                    ♡ —
                    ◇ A K J 5
                    ♣ A K
```

| WEST | NORTH | EAST | SOUTH |
|------|-------|------|-------|
|      |       |      | 2♣ |
| pass | 2◇ | pass | 2♠ |
| pass | 4♠ | pass | 6♠ |
| all pass | | | |

West leads the ♣J. How will you play the small slam in spades?

If trumps break 2-1, an elimination play beckons. You win the club lead and cash the ♠A, both defenders following. After cashing your second club winner, you cross to dummy with the ♠Q. Your idea now is to run the ♡Q to West, discarding a diamond from your hand. If West wins the first round of hearts, he will have only losing options available to him. A heart return will guarantee a trick for dummy's ♡J-10, on which you can throw your remaining potential diamond loser. West's only other alternatives will be to lead into the diamond tenace or give you a ruff-and-sluff.

When the cards lie as in the diagram, East will cover the ♡Q with one of his honors. What then?

It is time to switch tracks. You should ruff East's heart honor and continue with the ◇A, followed by the ◇5. If diamonds break 3-2, your worries are over. If East turns up with four diamonds, you can use dummy's last trump entry to finesse the ◇J. When the cards lie as in the diagram, West will have to win the second round of diamonds and he will be endplayed. As in the scenario we visualized before, a red-suit return will give you an extra trick and a club return will give you a ruff-and-sluff.

```
              ♠ 3 2
              ♡ 9 8 7 6
              ◇ Q J 7 4
              ♣ 7 5 2
♠ 6 5                        ♠ Q J 10 9 7 4
♡ —          N              ♡ J 5 2
◇ K 10 9 6 5 2  W   E        ◇ 8 3
♣ K J 10 9 3    S           ♣ 8 6
              ♠ A K 8
              ♡ A K Q 10 4 3
              ◇ A
              ♣ A Q 4
```

| WEST | NORTH | EAST | SOUTH |
|------|-------|------|-------|
|      |       |      | 2♣    |
| pass | 2◇    | pass | 2♡    |
| pass | 4♡    | pass | 6♡    |
| all pass |   |      |       |

West leads the ♠6 against your small slam. You win with the ace and draw trumps in three rounds, finding that West was void in the suit. You can ruff your losing spade. How will you try to avoid two club losers?

Suppose you ruff the third round of spades with the intention of finessing the ♣Q. West will show out on the third spade. What implications does that have? It means that West started with eleven cards in the minors to East's four. West is therefore an '11-to-4 on' favorite to hold the ♣K. The club finesse, which started out as a 50% chance, is now only a 27% chance. Justice is done when your club finesse loses. Down one!

How can you do better? You should cash the diamond ace before crossing to dummy with a spade ruff. When West happens to show out on the third spade, you switch tracks. You lead the ◇Q from dummy, intending to throw a club loser. East cannot beat dummy's queen (as you rather expected, when he holds only four minor-suit cards to his partner's eleven). West wins with the ◇K and is endplayed. Whether he plays a diamond to dummy's jack or a club into your ace-queen, the slam is yours.

# CHAPTER 10

# USE THE ENTRY WHEN A DEFENDER HAS TO DUCK

> *Use it or lose it*
> Mötley Crüe

There are many situations where a defender can thwart one line of play by holding up a high card. Sometimes you can wipe the smile off his face by making good use of the extra entry that the hold-up has given you.

## USING THE ENTRY TO TAKE A FINESSE

The auction 2NT–3NT often means that a fairly weak dummy will hit the table, with few entries on view. That was the case on this deal:

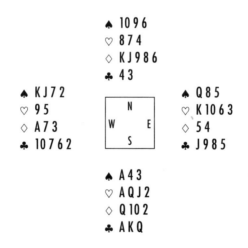

```
                    ♠ 10 9 6
                    ♡ 8 7 4
                    ◇ K J 9 8 6
                    ♣ 4 3
   ♠ K J 7 2                      ♠ Q 8 5
   ♡ 9 5             N            ♡ K 10 6 3
   ◇ A 7 3        W     E         ◇ 5 4
   ♣ 10 7 6 2        S            ♣ J 9 8 5
                    ♠ A 4 3
                    ♡ A Q J 2
                    ◇ Q 10 2
                    ♣ A K Q
```

| WEST | NORTH | EAST | SOUTH |
|------|-------|------|-------|
|      |       |      | 2NT   |
| pass | 3NT   | all pass |   |

How will you play 3NT when West leads the ♠2 to East's ♠Q?

Since you are well protected in the other three suits, you might as well hold up the ♠A for two rounds. You win the third round of spades and, as the opening lead of the ♠2 had indicated, the suit breaks 4-3. What now?

Unless the defenders are novices, you can bring in four diamond tricks only when the ◊A is singleton or doubleton and cannot be held up twice. Your first move should be to lead the ◊Q and overtake with dummy's ◊K. No ace appears on this trick. What is the prospect of the diamond ace being doubleton? It will happen on two-fifths of the 3-2 breaks, which is only a 27% chance. It is much more likely that the ♡K will be onside and you should therefore finesse the ♡Q next. When the cards lie as in the diagram, everything falls into place and the heart finesse will win.

Your next move is to lead the ◊10 and overtake with dummy's ◊J. Once again, the defenders will have to hold up the ◊A if they can. You can take advantage of this second entry to dummy to repeat the heart finesse. Even though hearts fail to divide 3-3, you now have the nine tricks you need: one spade, three hearts, two diamonds and three clubs.

## USING THE ENTRY TO CONTINUE PLAYING THAT SUIT

Sometimes a hold-up by the defender sitting over the dummy will allow you to finesse against his honor the next round of the suit. Look at the clubs here:

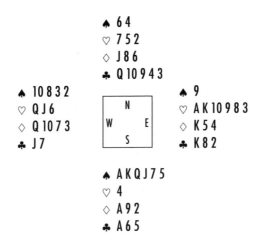

| WEST | NORTH | EAST | SOUTH |
|------|-------|------|-------|
|      |       | 1♡   | dbl   |
| 2♡   | pass  | 3♡   | 4♠    |
| all pass |    |      |       |

West leads the ♡Q against your spade game and continues with another heart. How will you play the contract?

You ruff and draw trumps in four rounds. If your next move is to play ace and another club, you will go down. East will hold up the king on the second round and you will have four unavoidable losers. Instead, you should play a low club to the ten on the first round. If East wins with the king, you will make four club tricks and score an overtrick. Let's suppose that East holds up the king. You can then take advantage of the entry to dummy by continuing with the queen of clubs. East does best to duck the ♣Q as well. You run the queen successfully, pinning West's jack, and score a third club trick with your ace. Ten tricks are yours: six trumps, three clubs and the diamond ace. You would make the same play in the simpler situation where dummy holds ♣Q-J-10-4-3.

(If East began with ♣K-x on the original deal, the winning continuation would be low to the ♣A on the second round. However, East is more likely to hold up with ♣K-x-x than with ♣K-x.)

## USING THE ENTRY TO TAKE A RUFF IN DUMMY

When dummy has a long side suit opposite a doubleton honor in your hand, the defenders may have to duck when you play the first round. This can give you an extra entry to your hand, allowing you to take an extra ruff.

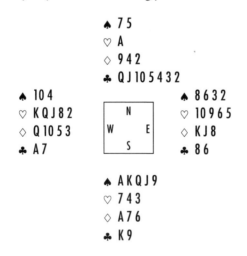

| WEST | NORTH | EAST | SOUTH |
|------|-------|------|-------|
| | 3♣ | pass | 4♠ |
| all pass | | | |

On a diamond lead, the play would be simple. You would win immediately, draw trumps and set up the clubs. The gods have given West an easy heart lead, however, and dummy's ♡A is removed at Trick 1. What now?

Unless the ♣A is singleton, the defenders will be able to kill dummy's club suit by holding up on the first round. Two heart ruffs would bring your total to ten, but you have only one quick side-suit entry to your hand (the ◇A).

Suppose you play a club to the king at Trick 2. What can West do? If he takes the ace immediately and returns a trump, you will score two overtricks. If instead West holds up the ♣A, you will have created a second quick entry to your hand. You can ruff one heart, return to the ◇A and ruff another heart. Provided the defenders cannot conjure a trump promotion with the fourth round of diamonds, you will eventually reach your hand to draw trumps and claim the contract. West's only other option is to win the first round of clubs and return a club. You will win with the ♣9 and again take two heart ruffs.

## USING THE ENTRY TO PREPARE FOR AN ELIMINATION

To prepare for an elimination, you need to remove at least one side suit from the battlefield. This may involve ruffing one or more rounds of a suit where dummy has length opposite a shortage in your hand. Look at the diamond suit here:

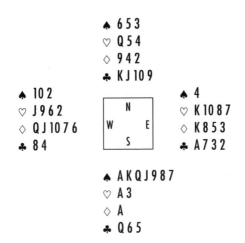

```
                    ♠ 6 5 3
                    ♡ Q 5 4
                    ◇ 9 4 2
                    ♣ K J 10 9
        ♠ 10 2                      ♠ 4
        ♡ J 9 6 2         N         ♡ K 10 8 7
        ◇ Q J 10 7 6   W     E      ◇ K 8 5 3
        ♣ 8 4             S         ♣ A 7 3 2
                    ♠ A K Q J 9 8 7
                    ♡ A 3
                    ◇ A
                    ♣ Q 6 5
```

| WEST | NORTH | EAST | SOUTH |
|------|-------|------|-------|
|      |       |      | 2♣    |
| pass | 2◇    | pass | 2♠    |
| pass | 3♠    | pass | 4◇    |
| pass | 6♠    | all pass |    |

West leads the ♢Q against your small slam. (You are right if you are think-ing that North overbid!) You win with the singleton ace and draw trumps in two rounds. What now?

It is a cruel blow that dummy's highest spot card in the trump suit will not provide an entry to the long club. Still, the defenders will have to duck the first two rounds of clubs and that will give you two entries to dummy. Can you make use of them?

After drawing trumps, you should play a club to the jack. East ducks, to prevent you from scoring three club tricks, and you take advantage of being in the dummy by ruffing a diamond. You continue with a club to the ten and East has to duck again. You ruff dummy's last diamond, eliminating that suit, and survey this end position:

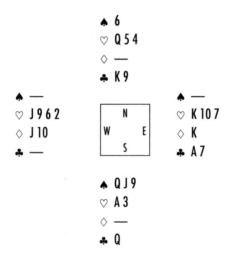

♠ 6
♡ Q 5 4
♢ —
♣ K 9

♠ —
♡ J 9 6 2
♢ J 10
♣ —

♠ —
♡ K 10 7
♢ K
♣ A 7

♠ Q J 9
♡ A 3
♢ —
♣ Q

When you lead the ♣Q, East has to win and then has no good return. The curtain falls on the deal as East explains to his partner exactly why an opening lead from ♡J-9-6-2 was the *obvious* move on his hand!

## USING THE ENTRY TO PREPARE FOR A THROW-IN

Even when the conditions are not present for a classic ruff-and-sluff elimina-tion, you may still be able to achieve a successful throw-in. On the next deal, the play is made easier by evidence acquired in the auction.

```
                        ♠ 6 4
                        ♡ K Q 8
                        ◇ 8 7 5
                        ♣ K Q J 7 6
        ♠ 7 5 2                         ♠ 9 8
        ♡ 9 3 2          ┌─────────┐    ♡ A J 10 6
        ◇ J 10 9 4 2     │    N    │    ◇ A 6 3
        ♣ 9 4           │ W     E │    ♣ A 10 5 3
                         │    S    │
                         └─────────┘
                        ♠ A K Q J 10 3
                        ♡ 7 5 4
                        ◇ K Q
                        ♣ 8 2
```

| WEST | NORTH | EAST | SOUTH |
|------|-------|------|-------|
|      |       | 1♣   | 1♠    |
| pass | 2♣    | pass | 4♠    |
| all pass | | | |

With only two spades in his hand, North might well have responded 1NT instead of 2♣. Still, a red-suit lead would have dispatched the alternative contract of 3NT. Defending 4♠, West leads the ◇J to East's ◇A. Seeing the threat that dummy's club suit offers, East switches smartly to the ♡J. His aim is to kill the heart entry to dummy. How will you continue the play?

You win with dummy's ♡Q and draw trumps in three rounds. Suppose you play a club next. East will note the ♣9 from his partner and hold up for one round. When he subsequently captures the second round of clubs, he will have a safe exit in diamonds and you will go down.

Before playing on clubs, you should cash the ◇K. You play a club to the king and East has to duck. The difference now is that you can take advantage of the entry to dummy. You can ruff a third round of diamonds, which will remove East's last card in the suit. When East wins the second round of clubs, he will have no diamond to play. He will have to return a heart or a club and the contract is yours.

We glossed over one important point in the description of the play. Can you think what it was? When you draw the third round of trumps, you must throw a club from dummy. If you carelessly discard dummy's last diamond, you will not be able to take the all-important diamond ruff to remove East's exit card.

## USING THE ENTRY TO CASH A WINNER

On the next deal, you must use the enforced entry for an unusual purpose: to cash a winner that will carry you past the finishing post.

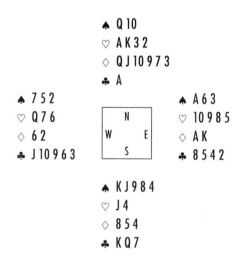

| WEST | NORTH | EAST | SOUTH |
|------|-------|------|-------|
| | 1♦ | pass | 1♠ |
| pass | 2♡ | pass | 3NT |
| all pass | | | |

West leads the ♣J against 3NT. How will you play the contract?

Should you play spades or diamonds? Let's see what happens if you call for the ♠Q at Trick 2. East will hold up the ♠A and if you persevere with spades East will win and switch to hearts (he can tell from the ♣J lead that South holds the ♣K-Q). You can set up the diamonds, but you will never reach your hand to score more than one club trick. You will make four diamond tricks, two heart tricks and one trick in each black suit. Down one.

It is better to lead the ◊Q at Trick 2. East wins and switches to the ♡10, covered by the jack, queen and ace. What now? If you carelessly persist with diamonds, East will win and knock out dummy's last heart stopper. He will then be poised to cash out to beat 3NT when he takes his ♠A. So, the time has come to lead the ♠Q. East cannot afford to win the trick or you will score four spade tricks and also reach the two club winners.

When East ducks, you overtake with the ♠K, guaranteeing yourself an entry to your hand. You make use of this entry to cash just one more club trick, retaining a guard in the suit. Only then do you clear the diamond suit. You will make four diamonds, two hearts, one spade and two clubs.

## USING THE ENTRY TO AVOID AN HONOR BEING RUFFED

Finally, we will see a deal where you use the entry to lead towards an honor that would otherwise be ruffed.

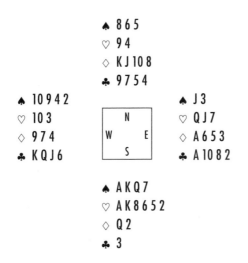

```
              ♠ 8 6 5
              ♡ 9 4
              ◊ K J 10 8
              ♣ 9 7 5 4
  ♠ 10 9 4 2              ♠ J 3
  ♡ 10 3          N        ♡ Q J 7
  ◊ 9 7 4     W     E      ◊ A 6 5 3
  ♣ K Q J 6       S        ♣ A 10 8 2
              ♠ A K Q 7
              ♡ A K 8 6 5 2
              ◊ Q 2
              ♣ 3
```

| WEST | NORTH | EAST | SOUTH |
|------|-------|------|-------|
|      |       | 1♣   | dbl   |
| 3♣   | pass  | pass | 4♡    |
| all pass |   |      |       |

West leads the ♣K against your heart game and continues with a second round of clubs, which you ruff. How will you play the contract?

Suppose you play the ace and king of trumps next. The suit divides 3-2, but you will still need a 3-3 spade break to make the game. East will, of course, hold up the ◇A for one round to restrict you to one diamond trick.

Instead, you should give yourself an extra chance by playing on spades while there is still a trump in dummy. Draw one round of trumps if you wish and then play the ace and king of spades. The idea now is to lead a third round of spades towards your hand. You play the ◇Q and overtake with dummy's ◇K. If East wins, you will be able to score two diamond tricks, discarding a spade. Let's suppose that East eyes his partner's count signal of the ◇4 and decides to hold up the ◇A for one round. You can then take advantage of the entry gained by leading a third round of spades towards your hand.

If East ruffs a losing spade, it will consume his natural trump trick and you will make the contract easily. East will do no better by refusing to ruff, however. You will win with the ♠Q and ruff your last spade in dummy. Whether East overruffs or not, the defenders will score just one trump trick and the two minor-suit aces.

**1**

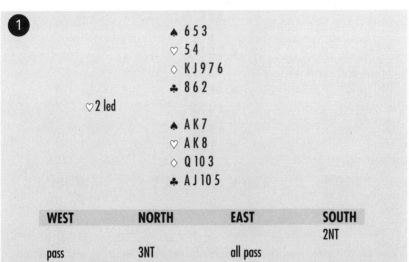

```
               ♠ 653
               ♡ 54
               ◇ KJ976
               ♣ 862

    ♡2 led

               ♠ AK7
               ♡ AK8
               ◇ Q103
               ♣ AJ105
```

| WEST | NORTH | EAST | SOUTH |
|------|-------|------|-------|
|      |       |      | 2NT   |
| pass | 3NT   | all pass |   |

West leads the ♡2 against 3NT, East playing the ♡J. How will you plan the contract?

**2**

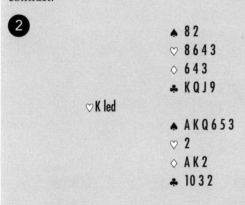

```
               ♠ 82
               ♡ 8643
               ◇ 643
               ♣ KQJ9

    ♡K led

               ♠ AKQ653
               ♡ 2
               ◇ AK2
               ♣ 1032
```

| WEST | NORTH | EAST | SOUTH |
|------|-------|------|-------|
|      |       |      | 1♠    |
| pass | 1NT   | pass | 4♠    |
| all pass |   |   |   |

West leads the ♡K against your spade game and continues with the ♡Q. You ruff and play the ace-king of trumps, West discarding a heart on the second round. How will you continue?

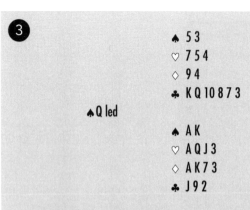

③

    ♠ 5 3
    ♡ 7 5 4
    ♢ 9 4
    ♣ K Q 10 8 7 3

♠ Q led

    ♠ A K
    ♡ A Q J 3
    ♢ A K 7 3
    ♣ J 9 2

| WEST | NORTH | EAST | SOUTH |
|------|-------|------|-------|
|      |       |      | 2NT   |
| pass | 3NT   | all pass |   |

You win the spade lead and play a club to the king, West playing the ♣5 and East the ♣4. How will you continue?

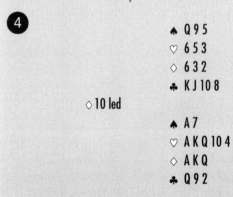

④

    ♠ Q 9 5
    ♡ 6 5 3
    ♢ 6 3 2
    ♣ K J 10 8

♢ 10 led

    ♠ A 7
    ♡ A K Q 10 4
    ♢ A K Q
    ♣ Q 9 2

| WEST | NORTH | EAST | SOUTH |
|------|-------|------|-------|
|      |       |      | 2♣    |
| pass | 2♢    | pass | 2♡    |
| pass | 3♡    | pass | 3♠    |
| pass | 4♣    | pass | 4♢    |
| pass | 4♡    | pass | 6♡    |
| all pass |   |      |       |

You win the ◇10 lead and cash the ace and king of trumps, West throwing a spade on the second round. How will you continue?

1

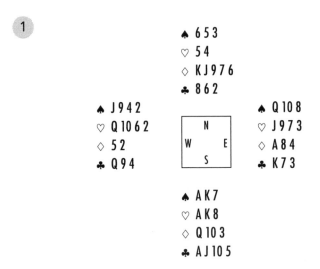

♠ 6 5 3
♡ 5 4
◇ K J 9 7 6
♣ 8 6 2

♠ J 9 4 2
♡ Q 10 6 2
◇ 5 2
♣ Q 9 4

N
W   E
S

♠ Q 10 8
♡ J 9 7 3
◇ A 8 4
♣ K 7 3

♠ A K 7
♡ A K 8
◇ Q 10 3
♣ A J 10 5

| WEST | NORTH | EAST | SOUTH |
|------|-------|------|-------|
|      |       |      | 2NT   |
| pass | 3NT   | all pass |   |

West leads the ♡2 against 3NT. How will you plan the play?

Noting that the lead of the ♡2 suggests that hearts are breaking 4-4, you win the first trick with the ♡A. You then lead the ◇Q to dummy's ◇K. East has to hold off, or you will score four diamond tricks. It is now safe to play a club to the jack. West wins with the club queen and persists with another heart. You win with the king of hearts and lead the ◇10 to the ◇J. Once again, East has to hold up the ◇A.

The diamond suit is dead, but at least it provided you with two entries to dummy. You finesse the ♣10, winning the trick. When the club suit breaks 3-3, you have three club tricks to go with two from each of the other suits. Game made!

```
                        ♠ 8 2
                        ♡ 8 6 4 3
                        ◇ 6 4 3
                        ♣ K Q J 9
        ♠ 4                             ♠ J 10 9 7
        ♡ K Q J 10 5      ┌───────┐     ♡ A 9 7
        ◇ Q 10 9 7        │   N   │     ◇ J 8 5
        ♣ 7 6 4         W │       │ E   ♣ A 8 5
                          │   S   │
                          └───────┘
                        ♠ A K Q 6 5 3
                        ♡ 2
                        ◇ A K 2
                        ♣ 10 3 2
```

| WEST | NORTH | EAST | SOUTH |
|------|-------|------|-------|
|      |       |      | 1♠ |
| pass | 1NT | pass | 4♠ |
| all pass | | | |

West leads the ♡K against your spade game and continues with the ♡Q. You ruff and play the ace and king of trumps, West discarding a heart on the second round. How will you continue?

You must aim to score all three of the low trumps in your hand. You lead a club to the king, which East has to duck (otherwise, you will score three club tricks, disposing of your diamond loser). Taking advantage of the entry to dummy, you ruff another heart in your hand. When you play a club to the queen, East has to duck again. You lead yet another heart, East discarding, and ruff in your hand. You can then cash the ace and king of diamonds, bringing your total to ten tricks. You made six trump tricks and four winners in the minor suits.

No doubt you noticed that West's heart continuation at Trick 2 was very helpful to you. Had he switched to any of the other three suits, you would not have been able to score all three of the low trumps in your hand.

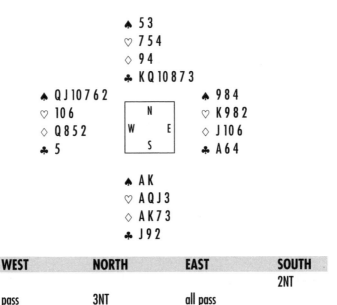

③

|  | ♠ 5 3 |  |
|---|---|---|
|  | ♡ 7 5 4 |  |
|  | ◇ 9 4 |  |
|  | ♣ K Q 10 8 7 3 |  |

| ♠ Q J 10 7 6 2 |  | ♠ 9 8 4 |
| ♡ 10 6 | N | ♡ K 9 8 2 |
| ◇ Q 8 5 2 | W   E | ◇ J 10 6 |
| ♣ 5 | S | ♣ A 6 4 |

|  | ♠ A K |  |
|---|---|---|
|  | ♡ A Q J 3 |  |
|  | ◇ A K 7 3 |  |
|  | ♣ J 9 2 |  |

| WEST | NORTH | EAST | SOUTH |
|---|---|---|---|
|  |  |  | 2NT |
| pass | 3NT | all pass |  |

You win the spade lead and play a club to the king, West playing the ♣5 and East the ♣4. How will you continue?

You have to choose between two lines of play. If clubs are 2-2, you can simply continue clubs. The ♣A will appear on the second round and you will score five club tricks, ending with an overtrick. The alternative is to finesse the ♡Q at this stage. If it wins, you can lead another club and repeat the heart finesse if the second club is also ducked. So, how do you compare the prospects for these two lines.

The heart finesse is a 50% prospect. What about a 2-2 club break? Initially, it was a 40% chance, but we can now rule out a 4-0 break (10%) and one quarter of the 3-1 breaks (where the ♣A is singleton, 12.5%). So, on the face of it a 2-2 club break is now a 52% chance. Does that make a second round of clubs the better line of play?

The calculation in the previous paragraph contains a serious flaw. Did you spot it? With dummy containing no side entry, the defender without the ♣A would surely give his partner a true count signal. The spot cards that appeared were the ♣4 and the ♣5. Neither defender has made a high-low signal from two low clubs, so it is virtually certain that clubs are 3-1! You should therefore take a heart finesse at Trick 3.

Although hardly any defenders would realize it, East does better to false-card the ♣6 on the first round of the suit. This robs you of the inference that clubs could not be 2-2.

```
                    ♠ Q 9 5
                    ♡ 6 5 3
                    ◇ 6 3 2
                    ♣ K J 10 8
      ♠ 10 6 4 3 2              ♠ K J 8
      ♡ 8             N         ♡ J 9 7 2
      ◇ 10 9 8 4    W    E      ◇ J 7 5
      ♣ 7 6 4           S       ♣ A 5 3
                    ♠ A 7
                    ♡ A K Q 10 4
                    ◇ A K Q
                    ♣ Q 9 2
```

| WEST | NORTH | EAST | SOUTH |
|------|-------|------|-------|
|      |       |      | 2♣    |
| pass | 2◇    | pass | 2♡    |
| pass | 3♡    | pass | 3♠    |
| pass | 4♣    | pass | 4◇    |
| pass | 4♡    | pass | 6♡    |
| all pass |   |      |       |

You win the ◇ 10 lead and cash the ace and king of trumps, West throwing a spade on the second round. How will you continue?

Your first task is to pick up the trump suit, so you lead a club to the ten. East has to hold up the ♣A or else you will use your next club entry to dummy to finesse in trumps and later discard your spade loser on the fourth round of clubs. Taking advantage of the entry to dummy, you finesse the ♡ 10 and draw East's last trump.

You continue with the ♣Q, which East again has to duck. Three rounds of diamonds extract East's cards in the suit. You cash the last trump, East throwing a spade, and then throw him in lead with a third round of clubs. He is forced to exit with a spade and you run this successfully to the queen.

(Suppose East had started with 2-4-4-3 shape. By cashing the last trump before exiting in clubs, you would squeeze him out of his safe diamond exit card.)

# CHAPTER 11

# USING A SIDE SUIT AS SUBSTITUTE TRUMPS

---

*Substitute*

The Who

---

The benefits of drawing trumps are well known. Sometimes, though, fate conspires against you and — for one reason or another — you cannot draw trumps. In this chapter, we will see how a powerful side suit can rescue you from this predicament. You use this side suit as 'substitute trumps'.

First, we will look at the situation where there is one trump still out, but you cannot draw it because you have no entry to the hand containing your master trump. You survive by playing substitute trumps (a long side suit) until the defender ruffs.

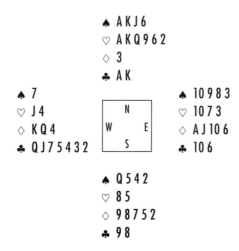

```
                  ♠ A K J 6
                  ♡ A K Q 9 6 2
                  ◇ 3
                  ♣ A K
  ♠ 7                             ♠ 10 9 8 3
  ♡ J 4              N            ♡ 10 7 3
  ◇ K Q 4      W         E        ◇ A J 10 6
  ♣ Q J 7 5 4 3 2       S         ♣ 10 6
                  ♠ Q 5 4 2
                  ♡ 8 5
                  ◇ 9 8 7 5 2
                  ♣ 9 8
```

| WEST | NORTH | EAST | SOUTH |
|------|-------|------|-------|
| 3♣ | dbl | pass | 3♠ |
| pass | 4NT | pass | 5♣ |
| pass | 5◇ | pass | 5NT |
| pass | 6♠ | all pass | |

North's 4NT was Roman Keycard Blackwood and the response showed no keycards. The 5◇ continuation asked if South held the queen of trumps, the 5NT response saying: 'Yes, but no side-suit king'. West leads the king of diamonds, followed by another diamond. You ruff the second diamond with the ♡6 and continue with the ace and king of trumps, discovering the 4-1 trump break. What now?

The trump suit is blocked. If your next move is to cash the ♠J, you will have no entry to the South hand to draw East's last trump. Leaving the ♠J in dummy as a potential entry, you turn to the heart suit, your substitute trumps. If East ruffs at any stage, you will overruff with the ♠Q and return to dummy's ♠J, drawing East's last trump, to enjoy the remaining hearts. If East declines to ruff, you will discard the two clubs in your hand, eventually continuing with the ♣A-K. East cannot score his ♠10 or ♠9, because you will overruff the moment he plays either of those cards.

## SUBSTITUTE TRUMPS TO REPEL A FORCING DEFENSE

A defender with four trumps headed by the ace will often embark on a forcing defense, because he knows he will have a second chance to force you (when he takes the trump ace). On the following deal, you can survive the force with the help of substitute trumps:

```
                        ♠ K Q 8 3
                        ♡ 9 4
                        ◇ A K J 8 2
                        ♣ Q 4
        ♠ 5                                 ♠ A 7 6 2
        ♡ K Q 10 5 3        N               ♡ A J 6 2
        ◇ 10 5 3      W          E          ◇ 7 6
        ♣ 10 7 6 2         S                ♣ J 9 3
                        ♠ J 10 9 4
                        ♡ 8 7
                        ◇ Q 9 4
                        ♣ A K 8 5
```

| WEST | NORTH | EAST | SOUTH |
|------|-------|------|-------|
|      | 1◇    | pass | 1♠    |
| pass | 3♠    | pass | 4♠    |
| all pass |   |      |       |

West plays king and another heart, won by East. How will you play when East continues with a third round of hearts, giving you a ruff-and-sluff?

East had an easy switch to a club. Why do you think he gave you a ruff-and-sluff instead? The most likely reason is that he holds four trumps to the ace. His plan is to force you to ruff in one hand or the other. He will then take his ♠A on the third round of the suit and force the last trump from the other hand. How can you withstand such a defense?

The answer is that you can use dummy's diamond suit as substitute trumps. However, you must take some care at Trick 3. Since East may hold only two diamonds, you should discard a diamond from the South hand and ruff in the dummy. You continue with the king and queen of trumps, not at all surprised when both cards are allowed to win and West shows out on the second round. These cards remain:

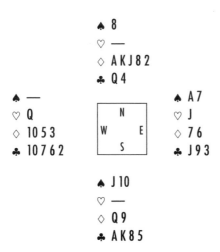

```
                    ♠ 8
                    ♡ —
                    ◇ A K J 8 2
                    ♣ Q 4
   ♠ —                           ♠ A 7
   ♡ Q              ┌─────────┐   ♡ J
   ◇ 10 5 3         │    N    │   ◇ 7 6
   ♣ 10 7 6 2       │ W     E │   ♣ J 9 3
                    │    S    │
                    └─────────┘
                    ♠ J 10
                    ♡ —
                    ◇ Q 9
                    ♣ A K 8 5
```

As discussed above, if you play another trump now, Easy will win and force your last trump with a heart. Instead, you should plan to run the diamond suit. There is one pitfall to avoid, though. If you simply play five rounds of diamonds, East will pitch his three clubs and subsequently ruff a club. So, you must cash a club winner (from either hand) before playing diamonds. East cannot counter this play. If he ruffs with the ♠7 at any stage, you will overruff and continue to play minor-suit winners.

On the next deal, the situation is more complicated. You must cope with a defensive holding of four trumps to the king-queen. With careful timing and some assistance from your substitute trumps, you can withstand the force.

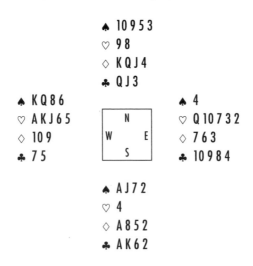

```
                    ♠ 10 9 5 3
                    ♡ 9 8
                    ◇ K Q J 4
                    ♣ Q J 3
   ♠ K Q 8 6                     ♠ 4
   ♡ A K J 6 5      ┌─────────┐   ♡ Q 10 7 3 2
   ◇ 10 9           │    N    │   ◇ 7 6 3
   ♣ 7 5            │ W     E │   ♣ 10 9 8 4
                    │    S    │
                    └─────────┘
                    ♠ A J 7 2
                    ♡ 4
                    ◇ A 8 5 2
                    ♣ A K 6 2
```

| WEST | NORTH | EAST | SOUTH |
|------|-------|------|-------|
|      |       |      | 1♣    |
| 1♡   | dbl   | 3♡   | 4♠    |
| all pass |    |      |       |

West launches the defense with the king and ace of hearts. You ruff the second heart, cross to the ♣Q and play a trump to the jack. West wins with the queen and has a choice of defenses. Suppose first that he exits passively with a diamond. You win with the ace and must take care with your next play. If you cash the ace of trumps, you will go down. When West wins the next round of trumps, he will be able to force dummy's last trump with another heart. Instead, you must lead the trump seven, retaining the ace in your hand. West has no counter to this. If he wins and plays a fourth round of hearts, you can ruff with the singleton ace and cross to dummy to draw West's remaining trumps with the 10-9. If instead West ducks, you will win in the dummy, draw a third round of trumps with the ace and run your minor-suit winners.

West's alternative line of defense is to lead a third heart when he wins with the trump queen at Trick 3. You discard a club from dummy, ruff in your hand and cash the ace of trumps, revealing the 4-1 trump break. West now has the K-8 of trumps, dummy has the 10-9 and your own trumps are exhausted. There is no point trying to draw West's trumps, because when he wins with the king, he will be able to force dummy's last trump with a heart. Instead, you must cross to the ♣J and continue with the king and ace of diamonds. (You need West to be 2-2 in the minors.) You now play the ace and king of clubs, your substitute trumps. West's trumps are neutralized. If he ruffs either club with a low trump, dummy will overruff.

## SUBSTITUTE TRUMPS TO REACTIVATE A TRUMP ENTRY

On the next deal, a bad trump break prevents you from 'drawing trumps, ending in the dummy'. The 'substitute trumps' cavalry will gallop to the rescue.

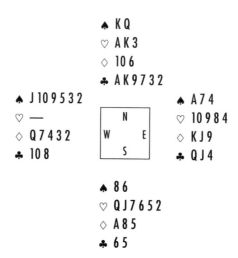

An auction of dazzling splendor carries you to 6♡. When West leads the
♠J, East wins with the ♠A and returns a spade. What is your plan?

You need to set up dummy's clubs, subsequently reaching the established
winners with a trump entry. If clubs break 3-2 and the trumps no worse than
3-1, you can ruff the third round of clubs high and return to dummy with a
third round of trumps.

At Trick 3, you play a trump to the queen. Bad news arrives when West
shows out, discarding a spade. What now? You play dummy's two top clubs,
everyone following, and lead a third round. East produces the outstanding club
and you ruff with a low trump. A trump to the ace leaves this position:

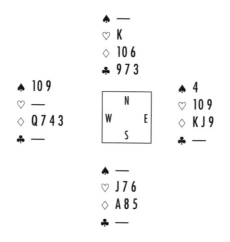

Dummy's club winners are your substitute trumps and East is powerless when you lead them. If he ruffs at any stage, you will overruff with the ♡J and return to dummy's ♡K, drawing East's last trump in the process. The slam is yours.

## SUBSTITUTE TRUMPS TO SURVIVE A 5-0 BREAK

Sometimes the situation is even worse and a defender holds more trumps than you do in either hand. Suppose you cannot afford to lose another trick and a defender holds two trumps, while you have one high trump in each hand. A desperate situation, yes, but you can sometimes survive. You play 'substitute trumps' until the defender ruffs. You then overruff and cross to the other hand to draw the last trump. That's what happens here:

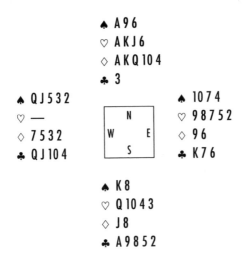

You reach a grand slam in hearts (nothing wrong with *your* bidding!) and West leads the ♣Q, which you win with the ace. How will you play the contract?

There are twelve top tricks and you can easily bump this to thirteen by taking a black-suit ruff in one hand or the other. The only risk to the contract is a 5-0 trump break. Do you have an idea how you might counter such a piece of bad luck?

On some deals you might attempt a crossruff. After one round of trumps, discovering the 5-0 break, you would need to cash six side-suit winners and then score the remaining six trumps separately by ruffing. This would be possible only against a very specific shape of the defenders' hands.

Here you have a powerful side suit in diamonds and it is better to play the hand by using 'substitute trumps'. Once you have discovered the 5-0 trump break, the general idea is that you will run the diamonds until the defender ruffs. You will then overruff and draw the remaining trumps. This will be possible only when it is East who holds the five-card trump holding.

At Trick 2, you must play the queen of trumps from your hand. When East turns up with five trumps, you play the king and ace of spades and ruff a spade. You then turn to your substitute trumps — diamonds, on this occasion. You will soon reach this end position:

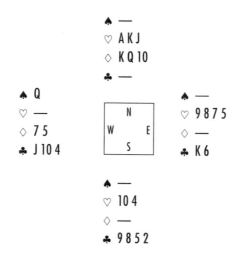

East has a disappointed look on his face. You continue to play diamonds and there is nothing he can do. Whenever he chooses to ruff, you will overruff with the ♡10 and draw East's remaining trumps with dummy's ♡A-K-J. Now you can see how important it was to draw the first round of trumps with an honor in the South hand.

What would happen if West were to show up with five trumps? You would then be forced to adopt the crossruff line instead.

## Substitute trumps to assist a trump coup

We will end the chapter with two deals where you use substitute trumps to perform a trump coup.

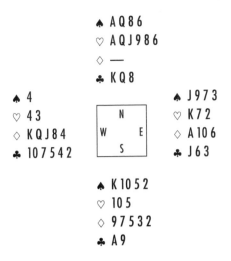

♠ A Q 8 6
♡ A Q J 9 8 6
♢ —
♣ K Q 8

♠ 4
♡ 4 3
♢ K Q J 8 4
♣ 10 7 5 4 2

♠ J 9 7 3
♡ K 7 2
♢ A 10 6
♣ J 6 3

♠ K 10 5 2
♡ 10 5
♢ 9 7 5 3 2
♣ A 9

| WEST | NORTH | EAST | SOUTH |
|------|-------|------|-------|
|      | 1♡    | pass | 1♠    |
| pass | 4♢    | pass | 4♠    |
| pass | 5♣    | pass | 6♠    |
| all pass |   |      |       |

West leads the ◇K against your spade slam. You ruff in the dummy and cash the ace and queen of trumps, West showing out on the second round. How will you continue?

Dummy's last trump is your sole protection from the opponents' diamond winners, so you must abandon the trump suit for the moment. The winning line is to continue with the ace and queen of hearts, forcing out East's king. East will probably continue with another diamond, which you have to ruff with dummy's last trump. You cannot draw East's trumps directly now, but you can run some hearts (your substitute trumps).

If East ruffs at any stage, you will simply overruff and draw his last trump before re-entering dummy in clubs. East does better to refuse to ruff, discarding two clubs. You throw your remaining three diamond losers to reach this end position:

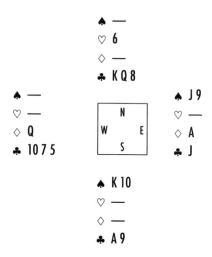

```
              ♠ —
              ♡ 6
              ◇ —
              ♣ K Q 8
  ♠ —                      ♠ J 9
  ♡ —         ┌─────┐      ♡ —
  ◇ Q         │  N  │      ◇ A
  ♣ 10 7 5    │W   E│      ♣ J
              │  S  │
              └─────┘
              ♠ K 10
              ♡ —
              ◇ —
              ♣ A 9
```

Suppose you lead dummy's ♡6 at this stage. East will ditch his last club and be able to ruff the next trick. You must cash the ♣K before leading the last heart. East will then have no answer. If he discards the ◇A, you will throw the ♣A and remain in dummy to lead a club towards your trump tenace.

What would happen if East defended differently, returning a club instead of forcing dummy with a diamond? You would win with the ♣A and ruff a diamond yourself, proceeding with exactly the same line of play.

(Before moving on, look back at the full diagram for a moment. Did you consider a different line of play, crossing to the ♣A after two rounds of trumps so that you could run the ♡10? It may look tempting, but East can then defeat you by refusing to win with the ♡10! If you repeat the heart finesse, he can win and return a club, killing the last entry to dummy.)

In our final example, declarer found himself in a 5-1 fit with a 6-1 break against him. An unpleasant dream after dining too heavily? No, the deal arose in a game on the *Bridge Base Online* Internet bridge site.

```
                        ♠ 6
                        ♡ K 7
                        ◇ Q 4 2
                        ♣ 10 9 8 7 4 3 2
    ♠ 9                                      ♠ 10 8 5 4 3 2
    ♡ Q J 9 8 4 3         ┌─────────┐        ♡ 10 6 2
    ◇ J 10 7            W │    N    │ E      ◇ 9 8 3
    ♣ A K 6              │    S    │         ♣ J
                         └─────────┘
                        ♠ A K Q J 7
                        ♡ A 5
                        ◇ A K 6 5
                        ♣ Q 5
```

| WEST | NORTH | EAST | SOUTH |
|------|-------|------|-------|
|      |       |      | 1♣ |
| 2♡ | dbl | 3♡ | 4♠ |
| all pass | | | |

Your 1♣ opening was part of the Precision Club system, indicating 16
points or more, and North's double showed any hand with 5-7 points. 3NT
would have been a comfortable contract, but the task before you is to make 4♠.
West leads the ♣A and continues with the ♣K, allowing East to discard a diamond. West switches to the ♡Q and you win with the ♡A. When you play two
top trumps, West follows with the ♠9 on the first round and discards a heart
on the second round. How will you continue?

The fall of West's ♠9 opens up the possibility of a trump coup, with your
♠7 eventually being promoted. You continue with the ace and queen of diamonds to reach this position:

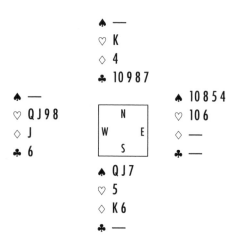

Dummy's club winners are your substitute trumps. When you lead the ♣10, East has no good answer. He cannot discard or you will throw a loser and continue with another club, certain to promote your ♠7. Nor can East ruff with the ♠4 or ♠5, because you will overruff with the ♠7, cash the ♠Q-J and play diamond winners, restricting East to just one trump winner.

Let's say that East tries to make life difficult by ruffing with the ♠8. You can now succeed in various ways. One of them is to overruff and play good diamonds. When East ruffs, he has two losing choices. He can lead a trump, allowing you to finesse, draw the last trump and claim the remainder. Alternatively, he can exit with a heart to dummy's king, allowing you to lead further substitute trumps to capture his remaining ♠10-5.

**1**

&#9824; K Q
&#9825; A K 8 7 5 2
&#9826; A 7 6
&#9827; A 6

&#9826; Q led

&#9824; A 10 9 7 5 3 2
&#9825; J 4
&#9826; 5
&#9827; 9 8 2

| WEST | NORTH | EAST | SOUTH |
|------|-------|------|-------|
|      |       |      | 3&#9824; |
| pass | 4NT   | pass | 5&#9826; |
| pass | 7&#9824; | all pass |  |

North bids a grand slam, hoping that you can set up his hearts to bring the total to thirteen. How will you play the contract? (You will soon discover that East holds &#9824;J-8-6-4.)

**2**

&#9824; A 2
&#9825; A K 2
&#9826; K Q J 6 4
&#9827; Q 8 5

&#9824; K led

&#9824; 10 8
&#9825; J 10 7 5 3
&#9826; A 2
&#9827; A K 6 2

| WEST | NORTH | EAST | SOUTH |
|------|-------|------|-------|
|      |       |      | 1&#9825; |
| 3&#9824; | dbl | pass | 4&#9827; |
| pass | 6&#9825; | all pass |  |

West leads the &#9824;K and you win with dummy's &#9824;A. You play the &#9825;A and West shows out, discarding a spade. When you play the ace, king and queen of diamonds, East ruffs the third round with the &#9825;8. How will you proceed?

1

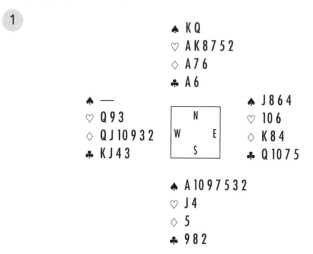

♠ K Q
♡ A K 8 7 5 2
◇ A 7 6
♣ A 6

♠ —
♡ Q 9 3
◇ Q J 10 9 3 2
♣ K J 4 3

N
W    E
S

♠ J 8 6 4
♡ 10 6
◇ K 8 4
♣ Q 10 7 5

♠ A 10 9 7 5 3 2
♡ J 4
◇ 5
♣ 9 8 2

| WEST | NORTH | EAST | SOUTH |
|------|-------|------|-------|
|      |       |      | 3♠    |
| pass | 4NT   | pass | 5◇    |
| pass | 7♠    | all pass | |

West leads the ◇ Q and your general hope is to draw trumps and set up the hearts. However, there is a chance of a trump coup when East holds all four trumps. You ruff a diamond at Trick 2, cross to the ♠ K and, lo and behold, West does indeed show out. You should ruff another diamond, cash the top hearts and ruff a heart. A spade to the queen leaves this position:

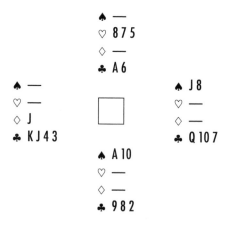

♠ —
♡ 8 7 5
◇ —
♣ A 6

♠ —
♡ —
◇ J
♣ K J 4 3

♠ J 8
♡ —
◇ —
♣ Q 10 7

♠ A 10
♡ —
◇ —
♣ 9 8 2

Let the substitute trumps roll! Dummy's hearts leave East powerless.

**2**

```
            ♠ A 2
            ♡ A K 2
            ◇ K Q J 6 4
            ♣ Q 8 5
♠ KQJ9753              ♠ 6 4
♡ —          N         ♡ Q 9 8 6 4
◇ 9 8 7 3  W   E       ◇ 10 5
♣ J 7          S       ♣ 10 9 4 3
            ♠ 10 8
            ♡ J 10 7 5 3
            ◇ A 2
            ♣ A K 6 2
```

| WEST | NORTH | EAST | SOUTH |
|------|-------|------|-------|
|      |       |      | 1♡    |
| 3♠   | dbl   | pass | 4♣    |
| pass | 6♡    | all pass |   |

West leads the ♠K and you win with dummy's ♠A. You play the ♡A and West shows out, discarding a spade. How will you proceed?

Aiming to dispose of the spade loser, you play the A-K-Q of diamonds. East ruffs the third round with the ♡8 and you overruff with the ♡10. West's likely shape is 7-0-4-2 and you continue with the three top clubs, followed by a club ruff in dummy. These cards remain:

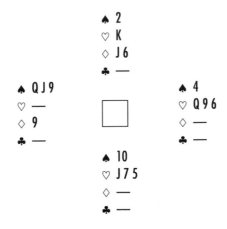

```
            ♠ 2
            ♡ K
            ◇ J 6
            ♣ —
♠ Q J 9              ♠ 4
♡ —                 ♡ Q 9 6
◇ 9                 ◇ —
♣ —                 ♣ —
            ♠ 10
            ♡ J 7 5
            ◇ —
            ♣ —
```

You lead the ◊J and East has no answer. If he ruffs with the ♡Q, you will discard your spade loser and make the rest. If he ruffs with the ♡9 or ♡6, you will overruff, cross to the ♡K and lead a diamond to promote your remaining trump. East's only other option is to discard the ♠4. You will discard the ♠10 and continue with another side-suit card from dummy, again leaving East with no way to defeat you.

## CHAPTER 12

# THE STEPPING STONE

*With a little help from my friends*
The Beatles

In this chapter, we will look at several deals where you can use a defender as a stepping stone to an otherwise inaccessible dummy. We will start with a relatively straightforward example:

```
                    ♠ 6 3
                    ♡ 8 6 5 3
                    ◇ 9 7 6 5
                    ♣ Q 8 3
   ♠ Q J 5                          ♠ 7 4
   ♡ K J 10 7          N            ♡ 9 4 2
   ◇ 4            W         E       ◇ Q J 10 8
   ♣ K J 9 5 2         S            ♣ 10 7 6 4
                    ♠ A K 10 9 8 2
                    ♡ A Q
                    ◇ A K 3 2
                    ♣ A
```

| WEST | NORTH | EAST | SOUTH |
|------|-------|------|-------|
|      |       |      | 2♣ |
| pass | 2◇ | pass | 2♠ |
| pass | 2NT | pass | 3◇ |
| pass | 4◇ | pass | 4♠ |
| all pass |  |  |  |

West opted for the fairly safe lead of the ♠Q. Declarer won in the South hand and drew a second round of trumps, everyone following. Take the South cards now. How will you continue?

Your contract will be at risk only if diamonds break 4-1 or worse. In that case it may be possible to endplay West with a trump. You should cash the ♣A and continue with the ace and king of diamonds. West may delay his predicament by refusing to ruff with his master trump, but it makes no difference. You will throw him in with a trump.

What can West do? A heart return will be into your tenace, giving you an easy tenth trick. Perhaps West will play the ♣K instead. In that case you will discard one of your diamond losers, leaving West on lead. He will then be forced to lead a heart into the tenace or play a club, allowing you to score the apparently stranded ♣Q in dummy. Game made!

Sometimes life is slightly more difficult. Try this one:

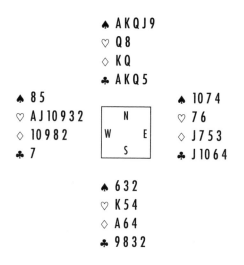

```
              ♠ A K Q J 9
              ♡ Q 8
              ◇ K Q
              ♣ A K Q 5
  ♠ 8 5                        ♠ 10 7 4
  ♡ A J 10 9 3 2      N        ♡ 7 6
  ◇ 10 9 8 2     W       E     ◇ J 7 5 3
  ♣ 7                S         ♣ J 10 6 4
              ♠ 6 3 2
              ♡ K 5 4
              ◇ A 6 4
              ♣ 9 8 3 2
```

| WEST | NORTH | EAST | SOUTH |
|------|-------|------|-------|
| 2♡ | dbl | pass | 3♣ |
| pass | 3♡ | pass | 3NT |
| pass | 6NT | all pass | |

With 0-7 points, South would normally bid a Lebensohl 2NT to show a weak hand. Since he held two prime honors, South ventured a semi-positive 3♣, suggesting a hand in the 8-10 point range. He was soon in 6NT, against which West led the ◇10. Declarer won with the ◇K in dummy and cashed two rounds of clubs, West discarding a heart on the second round. How would you continue from this point?

You must aim to strip East of his major-suit cards and then throw him in with a club, forcing him to give you access to the blocked diamond winner in the South hand. You cash dummy's five spade winners, followed by the ♣Q and the ◇Q. These cards remain to be played:

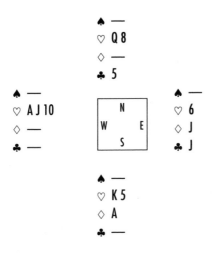

It's a pretty end position. 'Queen of hearts, please,' you say.

West has to duck this trick or you will cross to the ♡K to enjoy the ◇A. The East hand is now stripped of hearts. You throw him in with a club and he leads his last card, the ◇J, to your ◇A.

If East keeps both of his hearts, West has to keep a diamond guard, or you could just overtake the ◇Q. Now you lead the ♡Q from dummy and whether West wins this trick or not, he becomes the stepping stone to the stranded ◇A.

## STEPPING STONE IN AN ELIMINATION POSITION

Sometimes you have one entry to the dummy, but would like to bump this to two. On the next deal, your purpose is to repeat a finesse in a side suit.

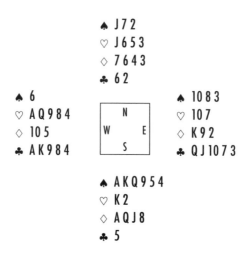

```
                        ♠ J 7 2
                        ♡ J 6 5 3
                        ◇ 7 6 4 3
                        ♣ 6 2
        ♠ 6                              ♠ 10 8 3
        ♡ A Q 9 8 4      ┌─────────┐     ♡ 10 7
        ◇ 10 5           │   N     │     ◇ K 9 2
        ♣ A K 9 8 4      │ W     E │     ♣ Q J 10 7 3
                         │   S     │
                         └─────────┘
                        ♠ A K Q 9 5 4
                        ♡ K 2
                        ◇ A Q J 8
                        ♣ 5
```

| WEST | NORTH | EAST | SOUTH |
|------|-------|------|-------|
| 1♡ | pass | 1NT | 4♠ |
| all pass | | | |

West leads the ♣K against your spade game, East playing the ♣Q to announce his sequence in the suit. West continues with a low club to East's ten and you ruff with the ♠4. All follow when you cash the ♠A. What now?

You should lead the ♠9 to dummy's ♠J. If trumps break 2-2, you will have two entries to dummy and can finesse twice in diamonds. As it happens, West shows out on the second trump, discarding a heart. You finesse the ◇Q successfully and survey this position:

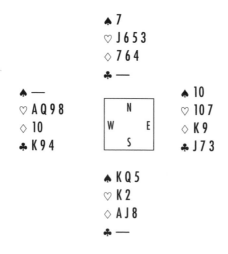

```
                        ♠ 7
                        ♡ J 6 5 3
                        ◇ 7 6 4
                        ♣ —
        ♠ —                              ♠ 10
        ♡ A Q 9 8        ┌─────────┐     ♡ 10 7
        ◇ 10             │   N     │     ◇ K 9
        ♣ K 9 4          │ W     E │     ♣ J 7 3
                         │   S     │
                         └─────────┘
                        ♠ K Q 5
                        ♡ K 2
                        ◇ A J 8
                        ♣ —
```

You would like to return to dummy to repeat the diamond finesse. You can use West as a stepping stone in this partial elimination position. When you play the ♡K, West has to win with the ♡A. He cashes the ♡Q and is then in some trouble. A diamond exit will do your work for you and a club exit will allow you to ruff in the dummy and repeat the diamond finesse. West's only remaining option is to play a third round of hearts. It will do East no good to ruff dummy's ♡J. You will then overruff and, thanks to your earlier unblock of the ♠9, be able to lead the ♠5 to dummy's ♠7. Your reward for all this hard work will be a chance to repeat the diamond finesse. The contract is yours.

## STEPPING STONE OR ENDPLAY

On the next deal, you can give West an unpleasant choice. Either he can act as a stepping stone to the dummy or he will be forced to open another suit, to your advantage.

```
                 ♠ K 10 5 3
                 ♡ 6
                 ◊ 9 7 5 3 2
                 ♣ 10 6 3
  ♠ 9 8 2                       ♠ Q J 7 6 4
  ♡ J 9 8 2         N           ♡ 7
  ◊ K Q J     W         E       ◊ 10 8 6
  ♣ K 7 4           S           ♣ Q 9 8 2
                 ♠ A
                 ♡ A K Q 10 5 4 3
                 ◊ A 4
                 ♣ A J 5
```

| WEST | NORTH | EAST | SOUTH |
|------|-------|------|-------|
|      |       |      | 2♣ |
| pass | 2◊ | pass | 2♡ |
| pass | 2NT | pass | 3♡ |
| pass | 3♠ | pass | 4♡ |
| all pass | | | |

West leads the ◊K and you win with the ◊A. When you draw two rounds of trumps, East discards a spade on the second round. What now?

Prospects are not particularly good, but there is some chance of endplaying West with the fourth round of trumps. First, you must strip him of his diamonds. You cash the ♠A and exit with the ◊4. West wins and cannot safely play a spade, a heart or a club. Like it or not, he has to return the ◊J. When East follows suit on this trick, a smile comes to your lips. You ruff in the South hand, cash a third top trump and put West on lead with his ♡J. He has a choice of two poisons. He can lead a club, giving you two tricks in the suit, or he can act as a stepping stone to dummy's ♠K. Ten tricks to you either way.

On the next deal, a defender can rescue his partner from being used as a stepping stone, but only at the expense of being endplayed himself.

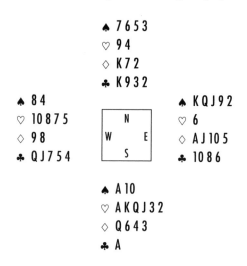

```
              ♠ 7 6 5 3
              ♡ 9 4
              ◊ K 7 2
              ♣ K 9 3 2
  ♠ 8 4                        ♠ K Q J 9 2
  ♡ 10 8 7 5      N            ♡ 6
  ◊ 9 8       W       E        ◊ A J 10 5
  ♣ Q J 7 5 4     S            ♣ 10 8 6
              ♠ A 10
              ♡ A K Q J 3 2
              ◊ Q 6 4 3
              ♣ A
```

| WEST | NORTH | EAST | SOUTH |
|------|-------|------|-------|
|      |       | 1♠   | dbl   |
| pass | 2♣    | pass | 4♡    |
| all pass |   |      |       |

West leads the ♠8 and you win East's ♠J with the ♠A. You draw trumps in four rounds, East throwing three clubs. What next?

You cash the ♣A, East throwing a spade, and exit with the ♠10. When East wins with the ♠J, he cannot afford to open the diamond suit and therefore returns a spade, which you ruff. Leading the ◇Q now is no good, because East will duck (to keep you out of dummy) and you will have no good continuation. Instead, you must lead a diamond to the king and ace. East exits safely with his last spade, which you ruff, and these cards remain:

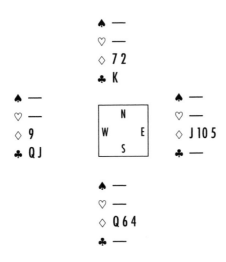

You lead the ◇4 and it is the defenders' turn to worry about a blockage! If West wins with the ◇9, he will have to act as a stepping stone to dummy's ♣K. If instead East overtakes with the ◇10, he will have to lead away from his ◇J-5 into your waiting ◇Q-6. You can send a few emails about this one when you get home!

## STEPPING STONE AFTER DEFENSIVE HOLD-UP

When a defender holds the ace of a long suit in dummy, he must often hold it up for a round or two to restrict declarer's communications. Sometimes declarer can get his revenge by using the defender's ace as a stepping stone. The next deal is unusual, because the long suit in question is the trump suit:

|           | ♠ 8 6 3           |           |
|           | ♡ Q 10 9 7 5 4    |           |
|           | ◇ A J             |           |
|           | ♣ Q J             |           |

| ♠ 9 7 5 4     |         | ♠ Q J 10 2    |
| ♡ A 8 3 2     |    N    | ♡ —           |
| ◇ 2           |  W   E  | ◇ 10 9 6 5 3  |
| ♣ K 10 8 5    |    S    | ♣ 9 7 4 3     |

|           | ♠ A K             |           |
|           | ♡ K J 6           |           |
|           | ◇ K Q 8 7 4       |           |
|           | ♣ A 6 2           |           |

| WEST     | NORTH | EAST | SOUTH |
|----------|-------|------|-------|
|          |       |      | 2NT   |
| pass     | 3◇    | pass | 3♡    |
| pass     | 5♡    | pass | 6♡    |
| all pass |       |      |       |

North's 5♡ is a general slam try, which South decides to accept. How would you play the contract when West leads the ◇ 2?

It looks normal, does it not, to win with the ◇ A and play a trump? If you do that, you will go down. West will hold up the ♡ A for two rounds and then exit with a spade. You will be stuck in the South hand with no way to reach the dummy to draw West's last trump. You would have to try a diamond to the jack and West would score a ruff.

There is only one way to make the slam. You must lead a spade at Trick 2! You will cash both your spade winners and then lead the ♡ J. West has to duck and you overtake with the ♡ Q, East showing out. You make use of the entry to ruff dummy's last spade with the ♡ K. After this indulgence of unblocking, the way is clear to lead the ♡ 6. West has to duck and you take the marked finesse of the ♡7. When you continue with the ♡10 to the ♡A, West has a three-way choice of how to give the lead to dummy. Suppose he plays a spade. You will ruff in the dummy and draw the last trump. You can then cash the ◊J and reach the remaining diamonds with the ♣A.

Suppose you are slightly inaccurate in your play and lead a trump to the nine after cashing the top two spades. It will cost you. You can ruff dummy's last spade with the ♡K, but when you lead the ♡J, West can duck to leave you stranded in the South hand. You cannot afford to overtake with dummy's ♡Q, because West would then score a trick with his ♡8.

On the next deal, you must combine two unusual techniques to make your small slam.

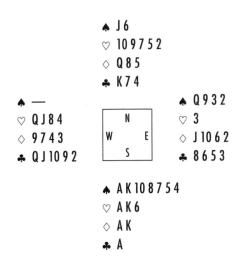

```
                    ♠ J 6
                    ♡ 10 9 7 5 2
                    ◊ Q 8 5
                    ♣ K 7 4
      ♠ —                          ♠ Q 9 3 2
      ♡ Q J 8 4          N         ♡ 3
      ◊ 9 7 4 3      W       E     ◊ J 10 6 2
      ♣ Q J 10 9 2       S         ♣ 8 6 5 3
                    ♠ A K 10 8 7 5 4
                    ♡ A K 6
                    ◊ A K
                    ♣ A
```

| WEST | NORTH | EAST | SOUTH |
|------|-------|------|-------|
|      |       |      | 2♣ |
| pass | 2◊ | pass | 2♠ |
| pass | 2NT | pass | 3♠ |
| pass | 4♣ | pass | 6♠ |
| all pass |   |   |   |

West leads the ♣Q against your small slam in spades and you win with the ace. How will you play the contract?

One possibility is to lead a low spade towards dummy. If West holds the queen of trumps, the jack will provide an entry to dummy and you will be able to reach the ♣K. It's only a 50% chance and, as the cards lie, you will go down. A much better idea is to lead the ♠10 from your hand. When trumps are 2-2 or 3-1, success is guaranteed (unless you are very unlucky and suffer a ruff). A defender who holds three trumps to the queen can either wave goodbye to his trump trick, by ducking, or he can capture the ten of trumps, thereby setting up the ♠J as an entry to dummy.

What will happen when you follow this line and the cards lie as in the diagram? East cannot afford to capture the trump ten or you will reach dummy and discard your loser. When the ♠10 is allowed to win, you can still succeed, provided East holds no more than two hearts. You continue with the ace and king of trumps, followed by top two diamonds and your two heart winners. If East ruffs the second heart, he will have to play one of the minor suits, giving dummy an entry and allowing you to discard your heart loser. If instead East declines to ruff, you will throw him in with a fourth round of trumps, to the same effect.

## THE STEPPING-STONE SQUEEZE

Finally, we will take a look at the stepping-stone squeeze itself. What are the hallmarks of this attractively named play? It will be easier to describe it if we look at a typical example first:

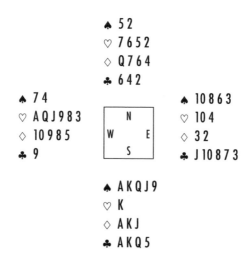

| WEST | NORTH | EAST | SOUTH |
|------|-------|------|-------|
|      |       |      | 2♣    |
| 2♡   | pass  | pass | 2♠    |
| pass | 2NT   | pass | 3♣    |
| pass | 3♠    | pass | 6♠    |
| all pass |   |      |       |

Reckoning that he would not pick up more than one 30-count in his life-time, South refused to stop short of a small slam. He leapt to 6♠ and West led the ♢10. How would you play the contract?

Declarer won with the ♢A, retaining the option to overtake in diamonds later in the play. He drew trumps in four rounds and tested the club suit, West showing out on the second round. All would be well if diamonds were 3-3, since declarer would be able to overtake on the third round. Another possibility was that West held four diamonds alongside the ♡A. He could then be caught in a stepping-stone squeeze. Declarer cashed his third winner in clubs and surveyed this end position:

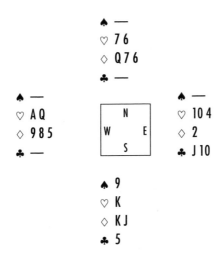

```
              ♠ —
              ♡ 7 6
              ♢ Q 7 6
              ♣ —
  ♠ —                      ♠ —
  ♡ A Q        N           ♡ 10 4
  ♢ 9 8 5   W     E        ♢ 2
  ♣ —          S           ♣ J 10
              ♠ 9
              ♡ K
              ♢ K J
              ♣ 5
```

When the last trump was led, West had an awkward discard to make. If he threw a diamond, declarer would be able to overtake on the third round of the suit, scoring his twelfth trick with dummy's fourth diamond. If instead West discarded the ♡Q, declarer would cash the two diamonds in his hand and throw West in with the ♡K to the ♡A, using him as a stepping stone to dummy's ♢Q. West's only other option was to throw the ♡A. This would beat the contract when East held the ♡K, but, as the cards lie, allowed South to score his ♡K.

This is the stepping-stone squeeze, then. Declarer has a blocked threat (in diamonds) which allows him to overtake if the defender releases his guard in the suit. He also has a one-card threat (the ♡K), which can lie in either hand.

Now, look back at the main diagram and imagine that East held four diamonds and four clubs. You could have caught *him* in a stepping-stone squeeze! The fifth round of trumps would have forced him to throw his last heart, retaining four diamonds and four clubs. You could then have cashed the ◇A-K-J and thrown East in with the fourth round of clubs to give dummy the ◇Q. (Yes, you could also have rectified the count by conceding a heart trick and then catching East in a simple squeeze. Still, who can resist a chance to show off at the bridge table?)

**1**

♠ 7 6
♡ 9 4 2
◇ K 9 8 6 3 2
♣ 7 6

♠ Q led

♠ A K 9 8 4 2
♡ A K J
◇ A
♣ A 5 3

| WEST | NORTH | EAST | SOUTH |
|------|-------|------|-------|
|      |       |      | 2♣    |
| pass | 2◇    | pass | 2♠    |
| pass | 3◇    | pass | 3♠    |
| pass | 4♠    | all pass |    |

West leads the ♠Q to your ♠A. When you duck a club, East wins and returns a trump to the king, West playing the ♠10. How will you continue?

**2**

♠ 9 2
♡ A K 9 7 6 3
◇ 6 5 3
♣ A K

♠ 6 led

♠ A 8 5 4 3
♡ 5
◇ A K Q J 10 2
♣ 6

| WEST | NORTH | EAST | SOUTH |
|------|-------|------|-------|
|      |       |      | 1◇    |
| pass | 1♡    | 1♠   | 2◇    |
| pass | 2♠    | pass | 3◇    |
| pass | 4♣    | pass | 4♠    |
| pass | 6◇    | all pass |    |

West leads the ♠6. You win with the ♠A and play the ◇A, not overjoyed when East discards a spade. How will you continue?

1

♠ 7 6
♡ 9 4 2
♢ K 9 8 6 3 2
♣ 7 6

♠ Q J 10          ♠ 5 3
♡ Q 8 5          ♡ 10 7 6 3
♢ Q 10 7 5       ♢ J 4
♣ J 9 4          ♣ K Q 10 8 2

```
      N
   W     E
      S
```

♠ A K 9 8 4 2
♡ A K J
♢ A
♣ A 5 3

| WEST | NORTH | EAST | SOUTH |
|------|-------|------|-------|
|      |       |      | 2♣ |
| pass | 2♢ | pass | 2♠ |
| pass | 3♢ | pass | 3♠ |
| pass | 4♠ | all pass | |

West leads the ♠Q and you win with the ♠A. When you duck a club, East wins and returns a trump to your king, West following with the ♠10. How will you continue?

You cash the ♢A and the ♣A and exit with a third round of clubs, hoping that West holds just three cards in the suit. If that is the case, the contract cannot be beaten. Suppose West wins the third round of clubs and cashes his master trump. He will then have to lead a heart into your ♡A-K-J tenace or act as a stepping stone to dummy's ♢K.

The defenders will not fare any better if East wins the third round of clubs. If he switches to a heart, you will rise with the ♡A and put West on lead with a trump, forcing him to give you an extra trick in one of the red suits. If instead East plays a fourth round of clubs, you will ruff in the South hand, knowing that West is endplayed if he overruffs. If he declines to overruff, you will throw him in with a trump on the next trick anyway.

**2**

```
              ♠ 9 2
              ♡ A K 9 7 6 3
              ◇ 6 5 3
              ♣ A K
♠ 6                            ♠ K Q J 10 7
♡ 10 2          ┌─────────┐    ♡ Q J 8 4
◇ 9 8 7 4       │    N    │    ◇ —
♣ J 9 8 5 4 2   │ W     E │    ♣ Q 10 7 3
                │    S    │
                └─────────┘
              ♠ A 8 5 4 3
              ♡ 5
              ◇ A K Q J 10 2
              ♣ 6
```

| WEST | NORTH | EAST | SOUTH |
|------|-------|------|-------|
|      |       |      | 1◇    |
| pass | 1♡    | 1♠   | 2◇    |
| pass | 2♠    | pass | 3◇    |
| pass | 4♣    | pass | 4♠    |
| pass | 6◇    | all pass |   |

West leads the ♠6 against your small slam in diamonds. You win with the
♠A and play the ◇A, not overjoyed when East discards a spade. How will you
continue?

If hearts break 3-3, it is an easy matter to draw trumps, establish the hearts
with one ruff and cross to dummy with a club to enjoy the long hearts. If
instead hearts are 4-2, two ruffs are required to set up the suit. You will then
need to use West as a stepping stone to the dummy.

You cross to the ♡A and cash the ♡K, discarding a spade. You then ruff a
heart high. On this trick West shows out, throwing a club. You return to
dummy with the ♣A and ruff another heart high, establishing two long hearts
in dummy.

The stage is set for the throw-in. You draw two more of West's trumps and
exit with the ◇2, forcing West on lead. He has only clubs left in his hand and
must give the lead to dummy's ♣K. The second of your spade losers goes away
and you cash dummy's two good hearts, disposing of your remaining losers in
spades. It's time to score up the slam.

# CHAPTER 13

# TWO-PART RECOVERIES

*Rescue me*
Aretha Franklin

In this chapter, we will look at some deals where you can succeed only by employing two different techniques. Your first task is to side-step an immediate threat to your contract. Can you then give your partner a 'you could rely on me, buddy' glance and reach for the next deal? Sorry, no. You must make sure that no further pitfalls await you.

To get you into the right mood, here is a gentle starter:

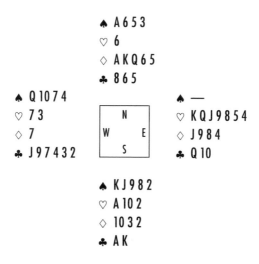

| WEST | NORTH | EAST | SOUTH |
|------|-------|------|-------|
| | | 3♡ | 3♠ |
| pass | 4NT | pass | 5♣ |
| pass | 5♠ | pass | 6♠ |
| all pass | | | |

Your 5♣ response shows 0 or 3 keycards. Since there is a miniscule chance that you hold no keycards, partner bids a disciplined 5♠, which you correct to 6♠. How will you play the slam when West leads the ♡7?

The immediate danger to the contract is that the trumps may break 4-0. It is very unlikely that East (the preemptor) holds four spades and, after winning the diamond lead, you should play the ♠K on the first round. When East shows out, you continue with the ♠J, covered by the ♠Q and the ♠A. Do you see any further problems that might develop?

It is not possible to ruff both heart losers in the dummy because West would ruff in with the ♠7 on the third round. All will be well, though, if diamonds break 3-2, because the suit will provide two discards. The extra chance you must play for is that East holds four diamonds and can be squeezed in the red suits.

You cross to the ♣A and ruff one of your heart losers. Then you play a trump to your nine and West's ten. Let's suppose that he exits with a diamond. You win in dummy, return to your hand with the ♣K and draw West's last trump with the ♠8, throwing a diamond (or a club) from dummy. These cards remain:

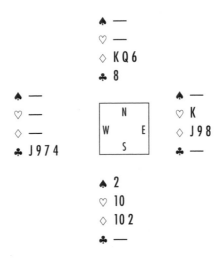

If you simply play on diamonds now, you will be disappointed. The suit breaks 4-1 and you will be left with a heart loser. Instead, you should play your last spade, squeezing East in the red suits. If he throws the ♡K, your ♡10 becomes good. If he throws a diamond instead, you will score all three of dummy's diamonds.

See if you can spot the two necessary techniques on the next deal:

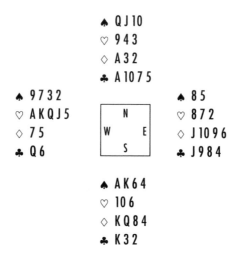

♠ Q J 10
♡ 9 4 3
◇ A 3 2
♣ A 10 7 5

♠ 9 7 3 2
♡ A K Q J 5
◇ 7 5
♣ Q 6

♠ 8 5
♡ 8 7 2
◇ J 10 9 6
♣ J 9 8 4

♠ A K 6 4
♡ 10 6
◇ K Q 8 4
♣ K 3 2

| WEST | NORTH | EAST | SOUTH |
|------|-------|------|-------|
|      |       |      | 1NT   |
| 2♡   | dbl   | pass | 2♠    |
| pass | 3♡    | pass | 4◇    |
| pass | 4♠    | all pass |    |

The bidding develops awkwardly and you end in a 4-3 spade fit. How will you play the contract when West leads the king and ace of hearts, followed by the queen of hearts?

Easily the best move at Trick 3 is to discard a club from the South hand. You preserve your four-card trump length and prevent West from doing any further damage with heart leads. (If he leads a fourth round of hearts, you can ruff in dummy and discard a diamond from the South hand.)

Let's suppose that West switches to a trump at Trick 4. What now? You should win and draw two more rounds of trumps. If trumps break 3-3, you will have the chance to play ace, king and another club, ruffing in the South hand. You will then make the contract when either minor suit breaks 3-3.

When the cards lie as in the diagram, West will turn up with four trumps. No matter! This will be the position with one trump still to be played:

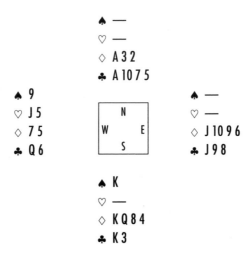

When you draw West's last trump, East is squeezed in the minor suits. Your tenth trick will come from whichever suit he decides to abandon.

We will look next at a deal where you can recover from a bad break only by scoring tricks from two different suits. You can perform this 'drawing from two wells' only by careful play in the first of the two suits.

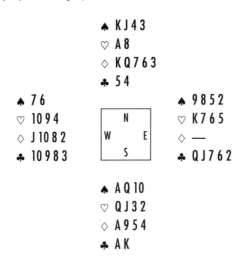

| WEST | NORTH | EAST | SOUTH |
|------|-------|------|-------|
|      |       |      | 2NT   |
| pass | 6NT   | all pass |   |

With adequate values for 6NT, North decides not to look for a diamond or a spade fit (a wise decision as the cards lie, since a small slam in the 5-4 diamond fit would be doomed by the bad diamond break.) West leads the ♣10, won with the ace, and a diamond to the king reveals the 4-0 split. How will you recover the situation?

There are ten top tricks. If West holds the ♡K, you can simply run the ♡Q. With the total up to eleven tricks, you could then concede a diamond trick, establishing your twelfth trick from that source. How likely is it that West holds the ♡K, though? West holds four diamonds to East's none, so the Law of Vacant Spaces suggests that East is more likely than his partner to hold the ♡K. Indeed, you can see from the diagram that East is longer than West in all three suits outside of diamonds. East is the favorite to hold a particular missing card in any of those suits. Can you make the slam when he holds the ♡K?

Once the bad diamond break has come to light, you should continue with four rounds of spades. This gives you further distributional information. West began with six cards in spades and diamonds to East's four. So, East is still the favorite to hold the ♡K.

You continue by leading the ♡8 towards your hand. East is caught in a Morton's Fork position. If he rises with the ♡K, he will give you a total of three heart tricks, enough for the contract. Let's assume that he senses this and plays low instead. You will win with the ♡Q, jump on your camel and head towards the other well — the diamond suit. You concede a diamond trick to West and then have twelve tricks. This last move would not be possible, of course, if you had played ace and another heart instead, releasing your control of the heart suit.

Moving swiftly on, we will see a deal where prospects appear to be good, until a diabolical trump break comes to light.

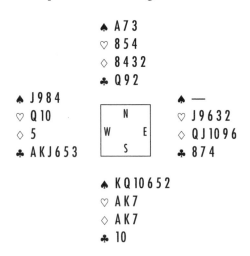

```
            ♠ A 7 3
            ♡ 8 5 4
            ◇ 8 4 3 2
            ♣ Q 9 2
♠ J 9 8 4                    ♠ —
♡ Q 10         N            ♡ J 9 6 3 2
◇ 5        W       E        ◇ Q J 10 9 6
♣ A K J 6 5 3      S        ♣ 8 7 4
            ♠ K Q 10 6 5 2
            ♡ A K 7
            ◇ A K 7
            ♣ 10
```

| WEST | NORTH | EAST | SOUTH |
|------|-------|------|-------|
|      |       |      | 1♠    |
| 2♣   | 2♠    | pass | 4♠    |
| all pass |   |      |       |

West leads the ♣K against your spade game. Judging from his partner's ♣4 that another top club would not be a good idea, West switches to the ◇5. You win with the ◇A and cash the ♠K, East discarding a heart. How will you attempt to recover from the 4-0 trump break?

East doubtless holds the sole guards on both red suits, but there is no chance of a squeeze. The squeeze card would have to come from the dummy (the hand opposite the red-suit entries) and the long trumps lie in the South hand. No, you must look for an endplay on West. You draw two more rounds of trumps with the ace and queen and then need to extract West's cards in the red suits. How are you going to do that?

Suppose you attempt to cash two winners in the red suit in which West has a singleton (diamonds, here). It will not be good enough. West will ruff with his master trump and exit in the other red suit. You will then lose one trick in each of the four suits, going down one. So, you need to read West's distribution in the red suits. What is your best guess?

The only clue is that you hold six hearts between the hands and seven diamonds. So, West is slightly more likely to hold a doubleton heart than a doubleton diamond. You cash the ♡A and, following the odds, continue with the ♡K. West follows suit — yes! The first part of your recovery, guessing West's shape, has been successful. These cards remain:

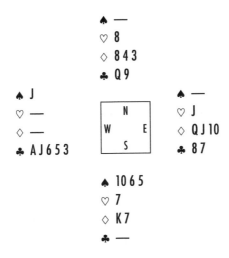

```
              ♠ —
              ♡ 8
              ◇ 8 4 3
              ♣ Q 9
  ♠ J                      ♠ —
  ♡ —          N           ♡ J
  ◇ —       W     E        ◇ Q J 10
  ♣ A J 6 5 3    S         ♣ 8 7
              ♠ 10 6 5
              ♡ 7
              ◇ K 7
              ♣ —
```

You now throw West in with a trump. He cashes the ♣A and you discard the ♡7. When he plays another club, you win with dummy's ♣Q and throw the other red seven. Your recovery is complete and the spade game is yours.

On the next deal, you must foresee the possibility of a bad trump break before playing to the first trick.

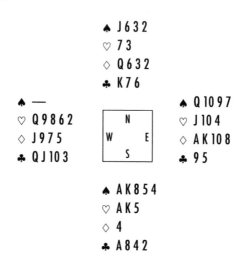

| WEST | NORTH | EAST | SOUTH |
|------|-------|------|-------|
|      |       |      | 1♠    |
| pass | 2♠    | pass | 4♠    |
| all pass |    |      |       |

West leads the ♣Q against your spade game. How will you play?

The contracts looks comfortable at first glance, since you can afford to lose a club, a diamond and a trump. Only a 4-0 trump break can cause any problems and you must address this possibility right from the start. Indeed, the first move to counter such a piece of bad luck must come right at Trick 1. You must win the opening lead in your hand, with the ♣A.

You play the ♠A next and West shows out, discarding a heart. How can you possibly make the contract now? You must aim to shorten the trumps in both your hand and the dummy. Your intention in the end position is that East will have to ruff at Trick 11 and then lead away from the ♠Q.

Your next move is to lead a diamond, preparing for diamond ruffs in your hand. East wins the trick and returns a club to dummy's king. You ruff a diamond and continue with the ♡A-K. A heart ruff returns you to dummy and you ruff another diamond in your hand. You have reached this end position:

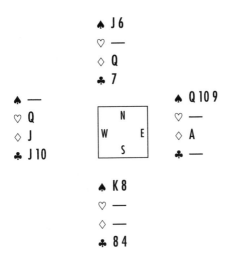

You exit with a club and West wins with the ♣10. It will not help East to ruff his partner's winner, so he discards the ◊A. When West continues with the ♣J, you discard the ◊Q from dummy and East is forced to ruff his partner's winning card. At Trick 12, he is forced to lead away from the ♠Q and you make the contract.

We will end with a couple of deals where you have to recover from your own bidding. It's usually so dependable, I realize, but on the present occasion, it has landed you in a less-than-ideal contract.

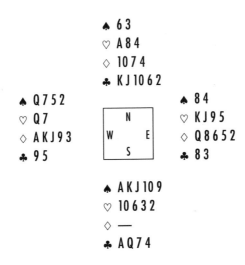

| WEST | NORTH | EAST | SOUTH |
|------|-------|------|-------|
|      |       |      | 1♠    |
| 2◇   | dbl   | 4◇   | 4♠    |
| all pass |   |      |       |

North is likely to hold four hearts for his negative double, but, sitting South, you decide to rely on your chunky spade suit. West leads the ◇K and down goes the dummy. A small slam in clubs would have had good play, yes, but how will you tackle the spade game?

You can afford to lose one trump trick, but you must be wary of losing control when trumps break 4-2. You ruff the diamond lead and the recommended first move in rescuing this contract is to lead the ♠10 from your hand. If this wins the trick, you will cash the ace and king of trumps and turn to the club suit. Suppose that West senses the position, leaps in with the ♠Q and plays another diamond. What now?

Now comes the second part of your plan. You discard a heart on the second round of diamonds and another heart on the third round. A fourth round of diamonds will cause you no problem, because you can ruff in the short trump holding with dummy's remaining trump. If West switches to a heart instead, you will win with the ♡A, draw trumps in three further rounds and run the club suit to dispose of your one remaining heart loser.

It has been an exhausting chapter and you will be relieved to hear that we are near the end. Are you ready for another dodgy 4♠ contract?

♠ K 8 6 4
♡ A 9 5
◇ K Q 4 2
♣ 9 3

| ♠ Q 10 9 | | ♠ J 7 |
|----------|---|-------|
| ♡ Q J 10 4 | N | ♡ K 7 3 |
| ◇ A J 10 7 | W    E | ◇ 9 5 |
| ♣ 8 6 | S | ♣ Q 10 7 5 4 2 |

♠ A 5 3 2
♡ 8 6 2
◇ 8 6 3
♣ A K J

| WEST | NORTH | EAST | SOUTH |
|------|-------|------|-------|
|      | 1♢    | pass | 1♠    |
| pass | 2♠    | pass | 4♠    |
| all pass |   |      |       |

West leads the ♡Q against your spade game. Something seems to have gone wrong with the formula 'opening bid + opening bid = game'. Since you have at least four apparent losers, you will have to take the club finesse in order to ditch a heart loser. You duck the first round of hearts and win the second with dummy's ace. A finesse of the ♣J succeeds and you cash the ♣A. When you continue with the ♣K, West ruffs with the ♠9. How will you proceed?

The first move is clear. West may have sacrificed a trump trick by ruffing and you should take advantage of this by discarding dummy's last heart. West has no wish to assist you by playing a diamond next, so he comes off lead with the ♡J.

There's no time for you to relax. Not only will you need to find the ♢A onside, you may also need to lead twice towards dummy's diamond holding. So, you must ruff the third round of hearts with dummy's ♠6, retaining the ♠4. You continue with the king of trumps and the ♠8 to your ace, pleased to see the remaining trumps break 2-2. These cards remain:

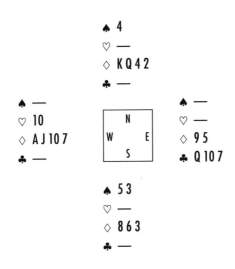

You lead a diamond to the king and, thanks to your previous unblocks of the ♠6 and the ♠8, can re-enter your hand with the ♠4, overtaken by the ♠5. A second diamond led towards dummy's ◊Q now gives you the contract. Your heroics should merit a "Well played!" from partner, at the very least.

**1**

> ♠ A 10 6
> ♡ Q 9 5 3
> ◊ A Q 7
> ♣ 6 5 4

◊9 led

> ♠ K Q 4 3
> ♡ A K J 2
> ◊ 6 5 3
> ♣ A K

| WEST | NORTH | EAST | SOUTH |
|------|-------|------|-------|
|  | 1♣ | pass | 1♡ |
| pass | 2♡ | pass | 6♡ |
| all pass |  |  |  |

You win the ◊9 lead with dummy's ◊A and play a trump to the ace, East showing out. How will you try to recover?

**2**

> ♠ 2
> ♡ Q 7 5 3
> ◊ K 10 8 7 4 2
> ♣ A 8

♠J led

> ♠ A K 10 9 8 6 4
> ♡ A 4
> ◊ A 9
> ♣ Q 6

| WEST | NORTH | EAST | SOUTH |
|------|-------|------|-------|
|  |  |  | 1♠ |
| 2♣ | 2◊ | pass | 3♠ |
| pass | 3NT | pass | 4♡ |
| pass | 5♣ | pass | 6♠ |
| all pass |  |  |  |

You win the trump lead and play a second trump, West showing out. When you play the ♠10 to East's ♠Q, he returns the ♣4. How will you continue?

1

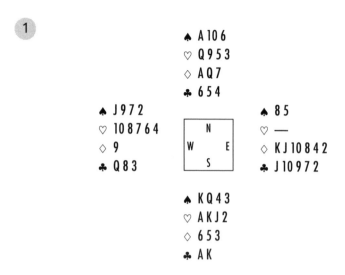

♠ A 10 6
♡ Q 9 5 3
◇ A Q 7
♣ 6 5 4

♠ J 9 7 2          ♠ 8 5
♡ 10 8 7 6 4       ♡ —
◇ 9                ◇ K J 10 8 4 2
♣ Q 8 3            ♣ J 10 9 7 2

♠ K Q 4 3
♡ A K J 2
◇ 6 5 3
♣ A K

| WEST | NORTH | EAST | SOUTH |
|------|-------|------|-------|
|  | 1♣ | pass | 1♡ |
| pass | 2♡ | pass | 6♡ |
| all pass | | | |

Not a believer in long auctions, you punt 6♡ on the second round. You win the ◇9 lead with dummy's ◇A and play a trump to the ace, East showing out. Ever felt unloved? How will you try to recover?

The first task is to enjoy four unruffed rounds of spades, allowing you to discard one of dummy's diamond losers. You need West to hold at least four spades and this makes him the favorite to hold the ♠J. So you cash the ♠K and finesse dummy's ♠10. The finesse wins and the sun continues to shine when you play the ♠A, East showing out. A trump to the king allows you to cash your last spade winner, discarding a diamond from dummy. What next?

If you concede a diamond trick immediately, you will go down. To time the play correctly, you must first cash the ace and king of clubs. That duty performed, you concede a diamond trick to East. Now nothing can prevent you from ruffing dummy's last club with your ♡J and scoring dummy's ♡Q-9, poised over West's ♡10-8.

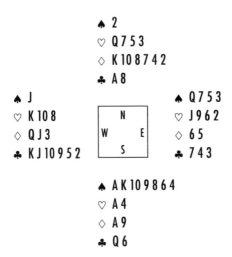

```
              ♠ 2
              ♡ Q 7 5 3
              ◇ K 10 8 7 4 2
              ♣ A 8
♠ J                          ♠ Q 7 5 3
♡ K 10 8        N            ♡ J 9 6 2
◇ Q J 3      W     E         ◇ 6 5
♣ K J 10 9 5 2     S         ♣ 7 4 3
              ♠ A K 10 9 8 6 4
              ♡ A 4
              ◇ A 9
              ♣ Q 6
```

West, who overcalled 2♣, leads the ♠J against 6♠. You win with the ♠A and cash the ♠K, West throwing a club. When you play the ♠10 to East's ♠Q, he switches to the ♣4. How will you attempt to rescue the situation?

There is no future in establishing the diamond suit, since the club switch has robbed you of a key entry to dummy. Instead, you must aim to catch West in a repeating squeeze. The first step is to preserve your ♣Q, winning the club switch with dummy's ace. You return to your hand with the ♡A and submit West to a torrent of trumps. This end position will arise:

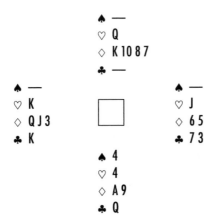

```
              ♠ —
              ♡ Q
              ◇ K 10 8 7
              ♣ —
♠ —                          ♠ —
♡ K                          ♡ J
◇ Q J 3                      ◇ 6 5
♣ K                          ♣ 7 3
              ♠ 4
              ♡ 4
              ◇ A 9
              ♣ Q
```

When you play the ♠4, West cannot afford a diamond discard, and if he throws either of his kings, you will play the established queen to squeeze him again!

# CHAPTER 14

# UNUSUAL WAYS TO RECTIFY THE COUNT

*Unusually unusual*
Lonestar

If you have battled your way through to the last chapter of this book, the chances are excellent that you already understand the idea of rectifying the count. You give up those tricks that you can afford to lose (one trick in a small slam, for example) to prepare the ground for a squeeze. The purpose is to tighten the eventual end position. You aim to leave a defender with no card to spare when you put him to a final discard.

In this chapter, we will look at some deals where the key play is the rectification of the count — sometimes in a manner that is not easy to spot. That said, we will start with a fairly straightforward example:

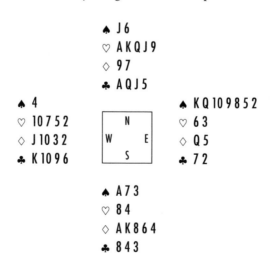

| WEST | NORTH | EAST | SOUTH |
|------|-------|------|-------|
|      | 1♡    | 3♠   | 3NT   |
| pass | 6NT   | all pass |   |

Partner allows you no leeway for your 3NT bid and raises directly to a small slam. How will you justify his faith when West leads the ♠4, East playing the ♠9?

Five heart tricks, four club tricks and the three pointed-suit winners will bring your total to twelve. West will need to hold the ♣K, yes, but a 3-3 club break is less likely than normal after East's preempt. You may therefore need a minor-suit squeeze against West to carry you past the finish line. How can you arrange this?

There is only one answer. You must duck the first trick, allowing East to win with the ♠9. You will win the ♠K return with the ace and finesse the ♣Q successfully. Next, you play your heart winners, arriving at this end position:

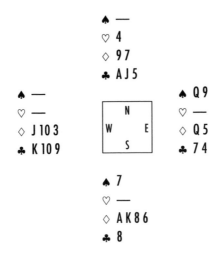

```
              ♠ —
              ♡ 4
              ♢ 9 7
              ♣ A J 5
  ♠ —                      ♠ Q 9
  ♡ —            N         ♡ —
  ♢ J 10 3   W     E       ♢ Q 5
  ♣ K 10 9       S         ♣ 7 4
              ♠ 7
              ♡ —
              ♢ A K 8 6
              ♣ 8
```

You play dummy's last heart, throwing the ♢6 from your hand, and West has no card to spare. If he throws a diamond, the ♢8 will give you the extra trick you seek. If instead West discards a club, you will cross to the ♢A and finesse the ♣J, setting up two further club tricks in the dummy.

On the next deal a skilled technician might foresee the potential end position even before playing his first card from the dummy. (He would be able to impress everyone by telling them this in the bar after the match.) See what you make of it.

```
                        ♠ Q 6 2
                        ♡ Q 9 3
                        ◇ A K 10 4
                        ♣ A K 2
        ♠ 9 4 3                         ♠ 7
        ♡ A K J 8 7 4    ┌─────────┐    ♡ 10 6 5 2
        ◇ 8              │    N    │    ◇ J 9 7 5
        ♣ J 10 3         │ W     E │    ♣ Q 8 7 5
                         │    S    │
                         └─────────┘
                        ♠ A K J 10 8 5
                        ♡ —
                        ◇ Q 6 3 2
                        ♣ 9 6 4
```

| WEST | NORTH | EAST | SOUTH |
|------|-------|------|-------|
|      | 1◇    | pass | 1♠    |
| 2♡   | dbl   | pass | 4♠    |
| pass | 5♣    | pass | 5♡    |
| pass | 6♠    | all pass |   |

North's double on the second round showed any hand with three-card spade support (a Support Double). South leapt to the spade game and two cue bids then carried the partnership to a small slam. How would you play 6♠ when West leads the ♡K?

There are eleven tricks on top and the only problem arises when East holds ◇J-x-x-x(-x). A declarer familiar with double squeezes will at this stage mutter to himself, 'West will have to keep the ♡A, East will have to keep the ◇J; no-one can keep a club guard.'

In case this is indeed the position, it is a good idea to rectify the count. There is only one safe way to do this. You must discard a club from your hand at Trick 1. (Suppose you were to ruff the first trick and duck a heart from dummy later, in an attempt to rectify the count. It would be no good. West would play a third heart to kill dummy's heart threat.)

So, you allow West's ♡K to win the first trick, throwing a club from your hand. Let's say that West switches to the ♣J. You win in the dummy, draw trumps in three rounds and play the ace and queen of diamonds to test that suit. When West does indeed show out on the second round, you can cash the ◇K and return to your hand with a heart ruff to run the remaining trumps. This is the end position that you might possibly have visualized when the dummy went down:

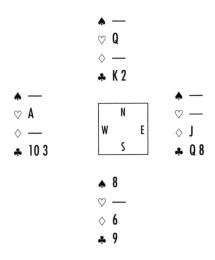

You lead the ♠8 and 'West has to keep the ♡A'. He throws a club and you discard dummy's ♡Q. 'East has to keep the ◇J, so no-one can guard the clubs'. The muttered mantra comes to pass. East has to throw the ♣8 and dummy's ♣2 duly scores your twelfth trick.

As you can see, it was not good enough to plan a squeeze once the bad diamond break came to light. You had to visualize that possibility at Trick 1, the only moment when it was possible to rectify the count safely.

## FORCING A DEFENDER TO WIN AND RECTIFY THE COUNT

Skilful defenders understand the importance of rectifying the count and will be reluctant to take an early trick against a small slam unless they are forced to do so. This is particularly true when the contract is 6NT. Sometimes you must play a suit in a particular way, to force the defender to take an early trick. If he fails to do so, you will score an extra trick by force. On the next deal, you intend to rectify the count in spades and must consider how best to play that suit.

```
                    ♠ Q 6 2
                    ♡ K Q 7 6
                    ◇ J 4 2
                    ♣ K 7 2
    ♠ A J 10 9 5 4          ♠ 8
    ♡ 9 4 3 2        ┌──────┐  ♡ 10 8
    ◇ 9 8 7          │  N   │  ◇ Q 10 6 5 3
    ♣ —            W │      │ E  ♣ 10 9 8 6 3
                     │  S   │
                    └──────┘
                    ♠ K 7 3
                    ♡ A J 5
                    ◇ A K
                    ♣ A Q J 5 4
```

| WEST | NORTH | EAST | SOUTH |
|------|-------|------|-------|
| 2♠ | pass | pass | 3NT |
| pass | 4NT | pass | 6NT |
| all pass | | | |

A spade lead from West would have been a reasonable choice against 3NT. Needless to say, it would be a very weak effort against 6NT and would have handed declarer the slam on a plate. Wisely seeking a safe lead, West reaches for the ◇9. Take the South cards now. How will you play the slam?

You have ten certain tricks outside spades and can develop an easy eleventh trick from the spade suit. So, all will be well, unless clubs divide 5-0. If East does indeed hold five clubs, you can squeeze him in the minors when he also holds the ◇Q. This is a near certainty after the ◇9 opening lead, so what can possibly go wrong?

I present to you the original declarer, who will demonstrate exactly what can go wrong. He won the diamond lead with the ace and, following what he regarded as general principles, led a low spade through West's ace. The contract could no longer be made! Unwilling to give declarer two spade tricks, West played the ♠9 on the first round. Dummy's ♠Q won the first trick, but when the bad club break came to light, there was no way to rectify the count for a squeeze against East. Declarer went through the motions, cashing four heart tricks, but East could spare two diamond discards and there was no way to make the slam.

Declarer made that most basic of mistakes — he failed to make a plan. Had he foreseen that a 5-0 club break was the only risk, or had he played the ♣A to check the lie of the suit, he would have turned his mind towards a possible minor-suit squeeze. The way to rectify the count for this is to lead the king of spades, rather than a low spade. West has to capture this card or you will score two spade tricks by force and make the slam easily. Once you have rectified the count in this way, you win the spade return with the ♠Q. You play the ◊K to free dummy's ◊J as an unfettered threat and then cash four heart winners. This will be the end position:

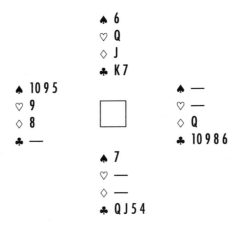

                    ♠ 6
                    ♡ Q
                    ◊ J
                    ♣ K 7
    ♠ 10 9 5                        ♠ —
    ♡ 9                             ♡ —
    ◊ 8          ┌──────┐          ◊ Q
    ♣ —          │      │          ♣ 10 9 8 6
                 └──────┘
                    ♠ 7
                    ♡ —
                    ◊ —
                    ♣ Q J 5 4

Dummy's last heart squeezes East in the minors and the slam is yours.

The next deal is similar, because you are forced to play for a squeeze only when one of your suits breaks badly. Take the South cards and see how you fare.

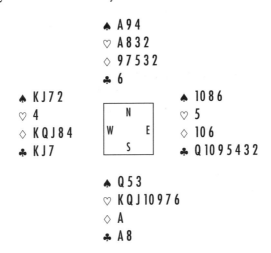

                    ♠ A 9 4
                    ♡ A 8 3 2
                    ◊ 9 7 5 3 2
                    ♣ 6
    ♠ K J 7 2                       ♠ 10 8 6
    ♡ 4          ┌──────┐          ♡ 5
    ◊ K Q J 8 4  │W    E│          ◊ 10 6
    ♣ K J 7      │   S  │          ♣ Q 10 9 5 4 3 2
                 └──────┘
                    ♠ Q 5 3
                    ♡ K Q J 10 9 7 6
                    ◊ A
                    ♣ A 8

| WEST | NORTH | EAST | SOUTH |
|------|-------|------|-------|
|      |       |      | 1♡    |
| dbl  | 4♣    | pass | 4NT   |
| pass | 5♡    | pass | 6♡    |
| all pass |   |      |       |

South won't win a bidding prize for the auction but — you never know — he may have a chance to shine in the play. How will you play the South cards when the ◇K is led?

If diamonds break 4-3, there are enough entries to establish the suit and take a discard on the thirteenth card. You win the first trick with the ◇A, draw the enemy trumps with the ♡K, cash the ♣A and ruff a club. When you ruff a diamond in your hand, an unwelcome ◇10 from East warns you that perhaps the diamonds are not 4-3. When you overtake the ♡9 with the ♡A and lead another diamond, East does indeed discard a club. How will you continue?

You can no longer establish a long card in diamonds and must turn your mind towards a spade-diamond squeeze against West. It will not be possible to squeeze West down to ♠K-x and a master diamond, throwing him in with a diamond. The long trumps are in the South hand and there will be no entry to reach the intended throw-in card (a diamond). No, you must aim for a simple squeeze and that means you must rectify the count.

Think about this for a moment and you will realize that the only convenient moment to rectify the count is now! You discard a spade on the third round of diamonds and West wins the trick. He can exit safely with a top diamond, which you ruff, but he will have no answer when you run the trumps.

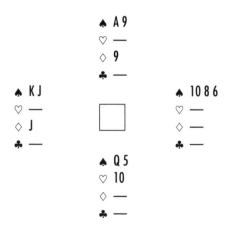

You lead your last trump and West has to throw the ♠J to prevent dummy's ◊9 from scoring. You discard the ◊9 from dummy and score the ace and queen of spades for the contract.

Let's look at something different — a deal where the trick on which you rectify the count has some bearing on which defender will be left guarding that suit.

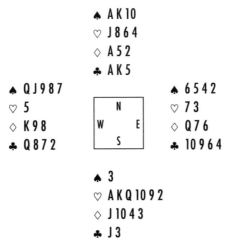

|  | ♠ A K 10 |  |
|---|---|---|
|  | ♡ J 8 6 4 |  |
|  | ◊ A 5 2 |  |
|  | ♣ A K 5 |  |
| ♠ Q J 9 8 7 |  | ♠ 6 5 4 2 |
| ♡ 5 |  | ♡ 7 3 |
| ◊ K 9 8 |  | ◊ Q 7 6 |
| ♣ Q 8 7 2 |  | ♣ 10 9 6 4 |
|  | ♠ 3 |  |
|  | ♡ A K Q 10 9 2 |  |
|  | ◊ J 10 4 3 |  |
|  | ♣ J 3 |  |

| WEST | NORTH | EAST | SOUTH |
|---|---|---|---|
|  |  |  | 1♡ |
| 1♠ | 2♠ | pass | 4♡ |
| pass | 6♡ | all pass |  |

West leads the ♠Q against your small slam in hearts. How will you play the contract?

You have eleven tricks on top and some chance of creating a twelfth trick directly from the diamond suit. If West held ◊K-x or ◊Q-x, for example, you could lead the ◊J from your hand. If West covered, you could win with the ◊A and lead back towards your ◊10. If instead West played low, you would run the ◊J and drop West's honor with the ◊A on the next round. Similarly, if East held a doubleton diamond honor, you could succeed by leading a low diamond from dummy on the first round, succeeding whether East rose with his honor or not.

There is no need to rely on such a chance. Provided the diamond honors are divided between the defenders, you can set up a double squeeze with clubs as the pivot suit. You draw trumps with the ace and jack and lead a low diamond from dummy. If East rises with his honor, you will have a finesse against West's honor. Since East in fact holds the ◊ Q, he is most unlikely to rise with the card. He plays low and your ◊ J forces West's ◊ K. Your play in diamonds has performed a dual role. It has isolated the diamond guard in the East hand and has also rectified the count.

Let's say that West returns the ◊ 9. You win with dummy's ◊ A, cash the ♠ K and run your remaining trumps, arriving at this end position:

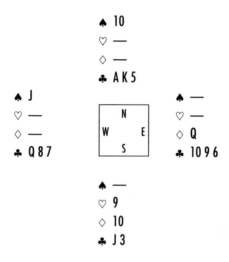

When you play the ♡ 9, West is the first to suffer. Since he has to retain the ♠ J, he must abandon his club guard. You release dummy's ♠ 10 and, if you enjoy putting opponents to the sword, turn to observe East in his plight. If he throws the ◊ Q, you will score the ◊ 10. If instead he abandons the club suit, you will score three club tricks in the dummy.

## RECTIFYING THE COUNT WITH A LOSING SQUEEZE CARD

Let's continue with a deal where you can rectify the count only after a certain amount of preparation. Once again you must recognize the possibility of a squeeze very early in the deal.

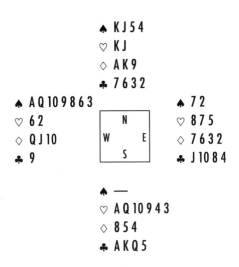

|  ♠ KJ54 |
|  ♡ KJ |
|  ◇ AK9 |
|  ♣ 7632 |

♠ AQ109863          ♠ 72
♡ 62                ♡ 875
◇ QJ10              ◇ 7632
♣ 9                 ♣ J1084

♠ —
♡ AQ10943
◇ 854
♣ AKQ5

| WEST | NORTH | EAST | SOUTH |
|------|-------|------|-------|
| 3♠ | 3NT | pass | 6♡ |
| all pass | | | |

Commendable brevity in the auction, yes, but how will you tackle the play when West leads the ◇Q?

There are eleven tricks on top and an easy twelfth will come from the club suit if it breaks 3-2. What if the clubs are 4-1? The opening lead of the ◇Q suggests that West may hold the sole guard in diamonds and may be susceptible to a spade-diamond squeeze. How can the count be rectified, though? If you simply draw trumps, test the clubs and give East a club trick, he will return a second round of diamonds to break up the squeeze.

The answer is to delay the club duck until near the end of the deal. Indeed, you plan to squeeze West on the very trick that rectifies the count!

How does the play go? You win the diamond lead with dummy's ace and draw one round of trumps with the king. You will need to extract East's spades for the eventual end position or else he could return a spade to West's ace when you duck a club. So, you ruff a spade, return to dummy with the ♡J and ruff another spade.

So far, so good. You now run your remaining trumps to reach this end position:

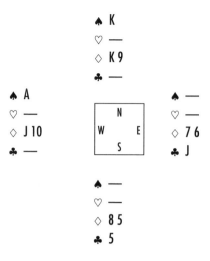

```
                    ♠ K
                    ♡ —
                    ◇ K 9
                    ♣ —
    ♠ A                           ♠ —
    ♡ —          ┌─────────┐      ♡ —
    ◇ J 10       │    N    │      ◇ 7 6
    ♣ —          │ W     E │      ♣ J
                 │    S    │
                 └─────────┘
                    ♠ —
                    ♡ —
                    ◇ 8 5
                    ♣ 5
```

You exit with the ♣5, rectifying the count and squeezing West at the same time. He has to throw the ◇10 to retain the ♠A and you discard dummy's ♠K. East wins the trick and, thanks to the two spade ruffs that you took, has no spade to play. He returns a diamond and dummy scores the last two tricks.

## LOSER-ON-LOSER RECTIFICATION

This deal is unusual because you rectify the count by leading a card you could have ruffed. You throw a loser instead and thereby tighten the end position.

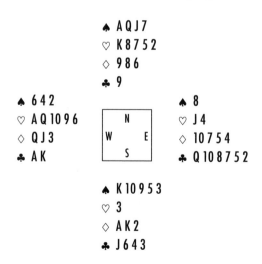

```
                    ♠ A Q J 7
                    ♡ K 8 7 5 2
                    ◇ 9 8 6
                    ♣ 9
    ♠ 6 4 2                       ♠ 8
    ♡ A Q 10 9 6  ┌─────────┐     ♡ J 4
    ◇ Q J 3       │    N    │     ◇ 10 7 5 4
    ♣ A K         │ W     E │     ♣ Q 10 8 7 5 2
                  │    S    │
                  └─────────┘
                    ♠ K 10 9 5 3
                    ♡ 3
                    ◇ A K 2
                    ♣ J 6 4 3
```

| WEST | NORTH | EAST | SOUTH |
|------|-------|------|-------|
| 1NT | 2♣ | pass | 4♠ |
| all pass | | | |

North's 2♣ overcall was Landy, showing both major suits. Not expecting his partner to hold much of value, West makes the intelligent lead of a trump against the eventual contract of 4♠. You win in the South hand, so that you can lead a heart towards dummy. West rises with the ♡A and plays a second round of trumps, won in the dummy.

Fondly imagining that you may be able to set up the heart suit, you ruff a heart in your hand. When you continue with a club, West wins with the ♣K and plays a third round of trumps. You win in dummy and ruff a heart, not pleased to see East show out. This is the position you have reached:

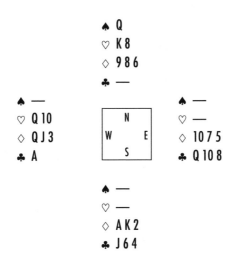

    ♠ Q
    ♡ K 8
    ◇ 9 8 6
    ♣ —

♠ —        ♠ —
♡ Q 10      ♡ —
◇ Q J 3      ◇ 10 7 5
♣ A        ♣ Q 10 8

    ♠ —
    ♡ —
    ◇ A K 2
    ♣ J 6 4

West guards the hearts and, very shortly, only East will guard the clubs. Your aim is therefore a double squeeze, where neither defender will be able to guard the diamond suit. Only two tricks have been lost so far, however, so the count has not been rectified. The moment has come to rectify that omission (no pun intended). You lead a club from your hand and the ace appears from West. Instead of ruffing in the dummy, you discard a diamond loser.

It makes no difference what West does next. Let's assume he returns the ◇Q. You win in your hand with the ◇A, leaving these cards to be played:

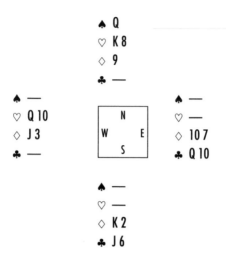

You lead another club. West has to keep both his hearts, so he must abandon his diamond guard. You ruff the club in dummy and cash the ♡K. East is squeezed in the minors and you will score your tenth trick in the suit that he abandons.

**1**

&spades; A Q 6 2
&hearts; A 5 3
&diams; 4 3 2
&clubs; K 10 6

&hearts;Q led

&spades; K 7 4
&hearts; K 10 7
&diams; A K 6
&clubs; A Q J 4

| WEST | NORTH | EAST | SOUTH |
|------|-------|------|-------|
| 3&hearts; | pass | pass | 3NT |
| pass | 4NT | pass | 6NT |
| all pass | | | |

West leads the &hearts;Q against 6NT. East discards a spade and you win with the &hearts;K. You play three rounds of clubs and the suit breaks 3-3. What now?

**2**

&spades; K Q 6 2
&hearts; A K 8 4 2
&diams; 9 6 2
&clubs; 7

&clubs;6 led

&spades; A 4 3
&hearts; 9 7 6
&diams; K J 10 8 4
&clubs; Q 2

| WEST | NORTH | EAST | SOUTH |
|------|-------|------|-------|
| | 1&hearts; | pass | 1NT |
| 2&clubs; | pass | 3&clubs; | 3&diams; |
| all pass | | | |

West leads the &clubs;6 to East's ace and back comes the &diams;5. When you play low from your hand, West wins with the &diams;Q and continues with ace and another trump, removing dummy's trump holding. How will you continue?

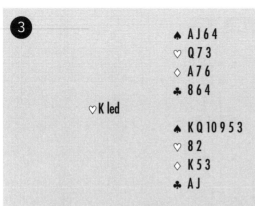

③

```
                        ♠ A J 6 4
                        ♡ Q 7 3
                        ◇ A 7 6
                        ♣ 8 6 4
        ♡K led

                        ♠ K Q 10 9 5 3
                        ♡ 8 2
                        ◇ K 5 3
                        ♣ A J
```

| WEST | NORTH | EAST | SOUTH |
|------|-------|------|-------|
| 2♡ | pass | pass | 2♠ |
| pass | 4♠ | all pass | |

West leads the ♡K, cashes the ♡A and lead a third round of hearts, which East ruffs with the ♠2. What is your plan for the contract?

④

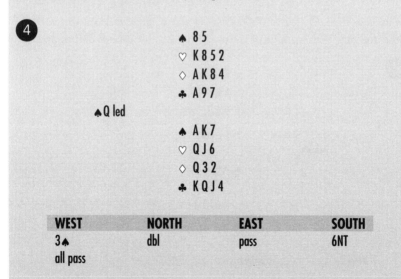

```
                        ♠ 8 5
                        ♡ K 8 5 2
                        ◇ A K 8 4
                        ♣ A 9 7
        ♠Q led

                        ♠ A K 7
                        ♡ Q J 6
                        ◇ Q 3 2
                        ♣ K Q J 4
```

| WEST | NORTH | EAST | SOUTH |
|------|-------|------|-------|
| 3♠ | dbl | pass | 6NT |
| all pass | | | |

West leads the ♠Q against 6NT and you win with the ♠A. There are nine tricks on top, with two more heart tricks readily available. A 3-3 break in either red suit will carry you past the finish line. Mind you, that's not likely in a chapter about rectifying the count. How will you play?

1

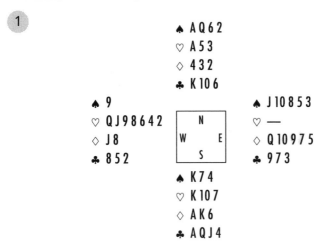

```
                    ♠ A Q 6 2
                    ♡ A 5 3
                    ◇ 4 3 2
                    ♣ K 10 6
♠ 9                                    ♠ J 10 8 5 3
♡ Q J 9 8 6 4 2      N                 ♡ —
◇ J 8          W         E             ◇ Q 10 9 7 5
♣ 8 5 2              S                 ♣ 9 7 3
                    ♠ K 7 4
                    ♡ K 10 7
                    ◇ A K 6
                    ♣ A Q J 4
```

West leads the ♡Q against 6NT. East discards a spade and you win with the ♡K. You play three rounds of clubs, the suit breaking 3-3. What now?

You have eleven tricks on top and will probably need a squeeze for the twelfth trick. West has already shown ten cards in hearts and clubs, so no squeeze will be possible on him. Instead, you must hope that East holds the sole guard in both spades and diamonds. You cash the ♠K and West follows suit. You still need to rectify the count. How can this be done?

You lead the ♡7, covered by West's ♡8, and must duck in the dummy. By surrendering a trick at this stage, you will extract one more card from the East hand. These cards remain:

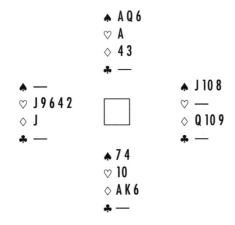

```
              ♠ A Q 6
              ♡ A
              ◇ 4 3
              ♣ —
♠ —                        ♠ J 10 8
♡ J 9 6 4 2                ♡ —
◇ J                        ◇ Q 10 9
♣ —                        ♣ —
              ♠ 7 4
              ♡ 10
              ◇ A K 6
              ♣ —
```

West's heart return, won in the dummy, squeezes East in spades and diamonds. If West exits with the ◇J instead, the pleasure of playing the ♡A squeeze card will be all yours.

```
                    ♠ K Q 6 2
                    ♡ A K 8 4 2
                    ◇ 9 6 2
                    ♣ 7
      ♠ J 9                        ♠ 10 8 7 5
      ♡ J 3            N           ♡ Q 10 5
      ◇ A Q 7      W       E       ◇ 5 3
      ♣ K 10 8 6 5 3    S          ♣ A J 9 4
                    ♠ A 4 3
                    ♡ 9 7 6
                    ◇ K J 10 8 4
                    ♣ Q 2
```

| WEST | NORTH | EAST | SOUTH |
|------|-------|------|-------|
|  | 1♡ | pass | 1NT |
| 2♣ | pass | 3♣ | 3◇ |
| all pass |  |  |  |

West leads the ♣6 to East's ace and back comes the ◇5. When you play low from your hand, West wins with the ◇Q and continues with ace and another trump, removing dummy's trump holding. How will you continue from this point?

The original declarer gave the deal insufficient thought. He played three rounds of spades, hoping for the 3-3 break that would allow him to discard his remaining club loser. Spades failed to divide evenly and there was no way to recover the situation.

There was little sense in declarer's line of play. If spades were 3-3, he would be able to throw his potential heart loser anyway. In the dangerous case where spades were not 3-3, it might be possible to make the contract on a major-suit squeeze. To this end, the correct play at Trick 5 is to lead the ♣Q, conceding a trick to rectify the count.

Suppose West wins with the ♣K and returns another club. You ruff with your penultimate trump and then cash dummy's ♡A-K to free your ♡9 as a threat card. You then return to the ♠A and play your last trump, throwing dummy's remaining heart. East has to find one more discard from ♠10-8-7 ♡Q. He will concede a trick, whichever card he chooses, and the contract is yours.

```
                    ♠ A J 6 4
                    ♡ Q 7 3
                    ◇ A 7 6
                    ♣ 8 6 4
    ♠ 8                           ♠ 7 2
    ♡ A K J 9 5 4    ┌─────────┐  ♡ 10 6
    ◇ J 8            │ W  N  E │  ◇ Q 10 9 4 2
    ♣ 10 7 5 2       │    S    │  ♣ K Q 9 3
                     └─────────┘
                    ♠ K Q 10 9 5 3
                    ♡ 8 2
                    ◇ K 5 3
                    ♣ A J
```

| WEST | NORTH | EAST | SOUTH |
|------|-------|------|-------|
| 2♡ | pass | pass | 2♠ |
| pass | 4♠ | all pass | |

West leads the king and ace of hearts, continuing with a third round of hearts, which East ruffs with the ♠2. What is your plan for the contract?

The only chance is to find that East holds the sole guard on both minors and can be squeezed. He will need to hold five diamonds and the ♣K-Q. Even then, you will not be able to squeeze him unless you have rectified the count. You have only one chance to do this and the moment is already upon you! You must discard a diamond from your hand at Trick 3, when East ruffs the third round of hearts.

Let's say that East returns the ◇10. You win with the ◇K, preserving dummy's ◇A as an entry, and run the trump suit. This position will arise:

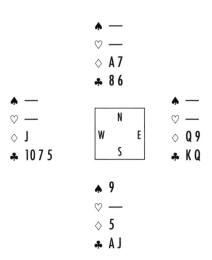

```
              ♠ —
              ♡ —
              ◇ A 7
              ♣ 8 6

  ♠ —                      ♠ —
  ♡ —         ┌─────────┐  ♡ —
  ◇ J         │    N    │  ◇ Q 9
  ♣ 10 7 5    │ W     E │  ♣ K Q
              │    S    │
              └─────────┘

              ♠ 9
              ♡ —
              ◇ 5
              ♣ A J
```

You lead the ♠9, throwing the ♣6 from dummy, and East is squeezed.

4

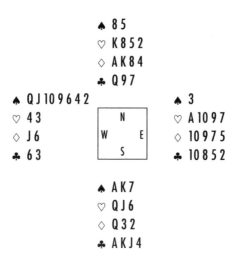

♠ 8 5
♡ K 8 5 2
♢ A K 8 4
♣ Q 9 7

♠ Q J 10 9 6 4 2
♡ 4 3
♢ J 6
♣ 6 3

♠ 3
♡ A 10 9 7
♢ 10 9 7 5
♣ 10 8 5 2

♠ A K 7
♡ Q J 6
♢ Q 3 2
♣ A K J 4

West, who opened 3♠, leads the ♠Q against 6NT. You win with the ♠A. There are nine tricks on top, with two more heart tricks readily available. A 3-3 break in either red suit will therefore carry you to victory. How will you play?

You cross to the ♣Q and lead a heart towards your hand. East cannot afford to go in with the ♡A or you will have three heart tricks and the contract. He ducks and the ♡Q wins. You re-enter dummy with the ♢A and lead another heart, the ♡J winning. You now test the lie of the cards by cashing the ♢Q and the ♣A. West follows all the way, marking him with 7-2-2-2 shape. This is the position you have reached:

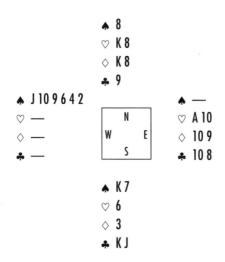

♠ 8
♡ K 8
♢ K 8
♣ 9

♠ J 10 9 6 4 2
♡ —
♢ —
♣ —

♠ —
♡ A 10
♢ 10 9
♣ 10 8

♠ K 7
♡ 6
♢ 3
♣ K J